Spence in 1963 at the height of his popularity as a university architect.

This book seeks to provide an introduction to the architectural work of Basil Spence. It has been written with an emphasis on his Scottish buildings and the earlier part of his career as an architect in Edinburgh. Spence never forgot his Scottish roots and developed an architecture of dramatic outline and robust appearance.

As, arguably, the leading architect of his generation Spence introduced the Modern Movement to towns and universities throughout Britain. His buildings and considerable skills as an orator prepared British taste for the sculptural and often alien forms of modern architecture. By respecting local building traditions and working with natural materials such as stone, Spence was in the organic tradition of twentieth-century architecture. By combining an architecture of strong geometry with local references Spence was able to soften the impact of his buildings. These techniques appealed to the general public rather more than to professional architectural critics who tended to find fault with the style and manner of his buildings.

Spence has had to suffer a generation of neglect and unpopularity. This book is an attempt to bring the works of Basil Spence into view. Regrettably the Spence family papers have not been available. As a result, the material examined relates mostly to buildings – ample evidence in many peoples' eyes of an architect's worth but limiting in terms of painting a fuller picture. Without drawing upon the full archive of personal detail, it is possible to present only a partial appraisal. As further details of Basil Spence and his family become available, other scholars can develop or adjust the arguments presented in these pages.

Brian Edwards

Brian Edwards 1994

Brian Edwards

Detail of bow window, 11 Easter Belmont Road, Edinburgh (altered in c.1970).

Introduction · An architect of pictorial eclecticism

Of the post-war architects, Basil Spence had a reputation for style and panache. His manner in both architectural work and speaking about architecture was vivid, persuasive, monumental and absorbing. In the committee rooms of the Royal Institute of British Architects (RIBA), on television and radio, Spence appeared as a man with a vision who had the energy and commitment to carry it into action. In an age when architecture was not part of popular consciousness, he made the subject appear important and exciting. Such was his stature that in 1962 he became only the second architect this century to receive Britain's highest honour, the Order of Merit. His OM and that awarded to Graham Sutherland (1960) and Henry Moore (1963) marked a high point in creative output in the post-war years.

Demand for building on a big scale in the aftermath of the Second World War was met by Spence who had in his personality the *'drama, tension and excitement'*[1] to produce buildings which matched the new social programmes. As Britain moved from austerity to prosperity in the late 1950s, Spence was one of the few British architects with the sense of mission and vitality to produce an architecture which coincided with the new mood of optimism. His many buildings and *'gleeful, high-spirited speeches'*,[2] his increasingly glamorous life as Britain's premier post-war architect, carried architecture to the world at large. He presented architecture as a concept in a fashion which had not been done before. His television appearances, his outspoken views, on the radio, in magazine interviews such as *Woman's Own*, as well as at many public engagements, provided Spence with the opportunity to prepare public taste for the new, daring designs which was to change the shape of towns throughout the country. Described by contemporaries as having charisma and never lacking personal courage, he carried the message of modern design to royalty, ministers, government departments and local councils.[3]

Massive state intervention to provide housing, schools, hospitals and university buildings in the 1950s and 1960s created unprecedented opportunities for British architects. The state at large and town councils locally became active not just in the provision of buildings, but in the restructuring of cities to accommodate new service industries and fresh modes of transport. Spence saw his task as that of more than a mere provider of buildings. He wished to prepare public taste for new architecture and to ensure, in particular, that government acted in an enlightened and progressive fashion. For two decades the example of his buildings and his many public remarks smoothed the transition from a culture which valued tradition to one which accepted, as a matter of course, the severe, linear forms of modern architecture. Coventry Cathedral was important in this respect. By being neither too abstract or modern in spirit, it prepared popular taste for the challenges ahead.

Spence was habitually busy, self-absorbed and impatient. He had a reputation for arrogance and becoming emotionally involved in the many issues which he chose to address. He made enemies both inside and outside the architectural profession. The inevitable march of personal ambition coincided happily with a period of economic growth when Spence was at the height of his powers both to speak for and to design new schemes. In Scotland particularly, the massive level of government investment in roads, housing, university and school building swept aside the perceived chaos and injustice of nineteenth-century capitalism.[4] Spence was one of the architects, along with Sir Robert Matthew, Robert Hurd and Sam Bunton, who gave the 'Brave New World' its physical form. Unlike his contemporaries, however, Spence *'seems to have made a conscious attempt, with his Romantic severity, to maintain a distinctively Scottish tradition'*.[5] Spence, almost alone among

The pedestrian view of the Gorbals blocks with their monumental concrete structure.

Brian Edwards

Quothquhan, 1938: Garden front.

architects in Scotland, sought to moderate the universal principles of modern architecture by locally generated concerns for the pictorial qualities of place, geographical location and building tradition. The specific nature of site and culture almost always balanced the dictates of formal architectural language and programmatic imperatives which were more generally the tenets of modern architectural design. These contextual concerns evident in the Canongate flats in Edinburgh and the more heroic Gorbals blocks in Glasgow, for example, allowed Spence to continue a tradition of pictorial eclecticism on the one hand and a powerful, essentially Scottish, rhetoric on the other. He was conscious that in the design of many of his buildings he was *'walking the aesthetic tightrope'* but admitted that he found it *'exhilarating'*.[6] The showman in Spence set him apart from contemporaries and helps to explain his attraction to later generations.

It could be argued that Spence's work in Scotland accurately mirrors the ebb and flow between 'Internationalism' and 'Empiricism' in his buildings elsewhere. In an age when the smooth, clean geometric shapes of the International Style were generally regarded as the true path of Modernism, Spence doggedly, and at times heroically, pursued a particularly personal style which incorporated local materials such as rubble stonework and textured render as well as sculptural forms. He exploited what he called the *'lusher pastures of plastic expression'*,[7] using light, silhouette, texture and internal volume for effect. At times, the artist in Spence coloured the more rational judgements needed of an architect, but the effect in Scotland and elsewhere was to leave a legacy of monumental structures where lesser architects left only buildings. Inevitably such heroics attracted many critics in his own time and later. The two twenty-storey slab blocks in the Gorbals elicited a mixture of admiration and condemnation. In

London, the Knightsbridge Barracks which overlooks Hyde Park was condemned in the House of Lords (see p.54). Lord Molson, former Minister of Public Buildings and Works, said, in 1972, that Spence would *'go down in history as the man who perpetrated the defacement of the Royal Parks'*.[8] The architectural press also turned against Spence in his final years accusing him of being too interested in the initial pictorial effect. By then the swing of the pendulum of popular and critical taste had moved measurably away from an architecture which placed the importance of individualism and expression to the fore. The emergence of the post-Modern ethos a generation after Spence's death has led to a reassessment of his work, particularly that aspect of his architecture which Peter Fawcett aptly describes as his *'mastery of form and composition within sensitive locations'*.[9]

Spence, described in his day as a *'gifted man not without a great sense of fun'*,[10] died deeply hurt by the injustice he felt over the rejection of many of his more conspicuous buildings. Sir Eric Lyons, President of the RIBA at the time of Spence's death, said that Spence had been grossly misjudged and unfairly criticised. Lyons, quoted in *The Guardian*, said that through his buildings Spence had tried to create richness and diversity for others to see. In seeking to push the expressive opportunities of architecture sometimes beyond the horizons of clients and the general public Spence was at least true to his principles, to the legacy of Le Corbusier whose debt Spence acknowledged, and also to Sir Edwin Lutyens in whose office he worked in his formative years.

The balance between the International and Empirical tendencies in modern architecture changed during Spence's life. In the 1930s the intellectual, if not the moral high ground, was held by the International Style under the influence of journals such as *Architectural Review*, but at the time of Spence's death in 1976, the less rational and more romantic

RIAS

Spence's first foray into high-rise housing. The perspective drawing, from March 1950, shows proposals for the new town of Newton Aycliffe, near Durham, designated in 1946 with a target population of 20,000. The design is a remarkably assured essay in cubic architecture with Spence's characteristic play of solid and spatial elements. It was prepared at the Edinburgh office.

*St Andrew Square, Edinburgh,
1960-2. Here the elevation is a
functional grid but notice the
articulation of entrance with its
double-height frame and the
maintenance of cornice lines.*

strain known as 'Empiricism' was in ascendancy. Spence was part of the shifting currents of artistic and professional taste, and helped smooth the transition from an arid, white Modernism of the pre-war years to a richer, more humane style of the 1950s. His *'fantastic fluency with words, draftsmanship and architecture',*[11] as Sir Hugh Casson put it, ensured that, whether in building or journalism, Spence was setting the agenda rather than following it. The conflicts of aspiration and priority are reflected in a lifetime's output of about one hundred and fifty buildings, of which a quarter are to be found in Scotland. These buildings mirror the innate tension between the universal values of 'Internationalism' and the need for architecture to respond to regional patterns of building, as well as to exploit sculptural expression. In his regard both for place and the importance of the pictorial concept, Spence was ahead of his time. With buildings such as Mortonhall Crematorium and the Canongate flats, Spence could use progressive modern influences yet at the same time keep in tune with local traditions and the aesthetic dictates of particular sites.

Flexibility in relation to design suggests that the Empiricist tendency was dominant in Spence, in the sense that the sensory, locational and visual experience of architecture took precedence over abstract geometries. But his buildings show more than that: he was a designer who articulated different moods and ambitions in response to a wide variety of clients and the distinctive qualities of sites. Two decades before such concepts were commonplace, Spence promulgated pluralism in architecture. He could design in an extravagant, sculptural, crisp and austere way, but nevertheless remain traditional at the same time. Few other architects have displayed such flexibility of outlook to place and programme, or such elasticity of architectural ambition. He represents the opposite pole to Peter Smithson in England or, perhaps from a later generation, Sir Richard Rogers or Sir Norman Foster.

The ability of Spence to express a kind of primitivist drama through the building programme recalls Le Corbusier at his poetic best between the years 1945 and 1965. Like Le Corbusier, Spence was intent upon *a complex interweaving of old themes and new forms of expression'*. The expressionistic wilfulness which some saw in Spence and which upset politicians such as Lord Molson rarely broke free of the intellectual refinement characteristic of the man. Even at Coventry Cathedral his bold architectural solution was checked by an innate regard for the old fabric, the principles of Gothic architecture and the liturgical needs of the congregation. Here Spence did not regress into feeble Mannerism (as many of the competitors did) but used structure, light and natural materials in a contemporary fashion as he was later to do at Mortonhall Crematorium in Edinburgh. As the American architectural critic Lewis Mumford noted of Coventry, the *'fusion of continuity and creativity strikes a note that vibrates longer and with deeper resonance than many other works of modern architecture'*.[12]

Such continuity and creativity are evident in many of Spence's buildings. The quality of light so skilfully engineered, the tactile impression gained by making a collage of materials, textures and colours, and the dextrous handling of space, all point to an architect of prodigious talent. The formal concerns of Spence to break the mould of simple linearity which was the central visual characteristic of modern architecture found expression in many of his buildings both in Scotland and elsewhere. Spence has been described as continuing the tradition in Scotland of pictorial eclecticism,[13] yet he was more generally preoccupied by greater architectural ambition. His terminal building at Glasgow Airport, Edinburgh University Library, the Gorbals blocks and Mortonhall Crematorium point to an architecture of considered monumentality – where shape, silhouette and internal volume interact dynamically. In this regard Spence maintained a British tradition whose roots extend back to the Renaissance, where architecture was the structure itself and not design ideas superimposed on a building. In Scotland such love of shape, silhouette and fine craftsmanship found expression in the architecture of the seventeenth century and were reinterpreted for the modern age through the buildings of Robert Lorimer and Frank Mears. Certainly, the education Spence received at Edinburgh College of Art in the 1920s would have instilled in him the importance of the picturesque and monumental traditions of Scottish architecture.

Spence is relevant today in one further respect. The balancing of international and national concerns which his buildings embody points to a future for Scottish, and more generally British, architecture. The blending of Scotland's tradition of masonry-based, monumental architecture with principles drawn from other countries produced, in Spence's hand, buildings of strong visual impact and intellectual weight. As early as 1960 Spence argued for a regionally distinctive architecture tailored to climate, social need and local geography. His was an architecture which looked to the north and to the south for sources of inspiration. Spence saw in the Nordic tradition a concern for climate and nature which could enrich the emerging Scottish pattern of building, and in the work of Continental masters, such as Le Corbusier and Auguste Perret, a southern, structural logic and spatial drama which were fitted to the tasks of the future. Few other architects of the period transformed a regional tradition into a progressive language. If Scotland in the 1990s is again caught in the cross currents of nationalism and internationalism, Spence teaches us that an authentic, visually rich and regionally distinctive architecture can emerge from the corpus of principles and design philosophy which lie at the root of the Modern Movement.

More than any architect of the post-war period Spence *'signalled the popular arrival of architecture'*.[14] He did so by achieving an effective marriage between the rigour and central discipline of Modernism, and formal mastery of architectural composition. His beautifully crafted buildings in both Scotland and England testify to a designer able to strike a balance between the picturesque and monumental, between functional expression and structural display. In an age when architecture was caught in a fight between what Leonard Manasseh, in his 1964 presidential address to the Architectural Association, called the 'Art Boys' and the 'System Boys',[15] Spence, along with Denys Lasdun and Eric Lyons, used both currents to turn buildings into major modern artworks.

RIAS

The University of Glasgow Institute of Genetics, 1966. Crisp silhouettes and powerful contrasts of solid and void make Spence's buildings into landmarks.

Chapter 1 · Education and practice in pre-war Scotland

RIAS Quarterly

Drawing of Château de Montainville from Spence's student sketchbook of 1928.

It was at the College of Art that Spence met William Kininmonth, later to become a good friend and partner, as well as Alan Reiach who also followed Spence to Rowand Anderson's office in Edinburgh. At the College, Spence came under the influence of important teachers and practitioners: the accomplished architect, town planner and a leader in the Scots Revival of the 1930s, Frank Mears was the senior lecturer in architecture; the historian John Summerson taught Spence design theory; and he was also instructed in design by Harry Hubbard, former chief assistant to Robert Lorimer, for whom Spence was subsequently to prepare presentation perspectives.

At the age of twelve, Basil Spence left the John Connon School in Bombay, India, to become a boarder at George Watson's College in Edinburgh. Spence, the son of an Indian Civil Servant had needed a scholarship to attend one of Scotland's finest fee-paying private schools.[1] He enjoyed an undistinguished six years leaving Watson's in 1925. Spence did, however, display sufficient talent to obtain a place at Edinburgh College of Art, initially to study painting and sculpture.[2] The combination of an intermediate school certificate awarded by Watson's and a portfolio of sketches was enough for Spence to be admitted into the joint foundation year at the College in September 1925. The architecture course shared classes with painters, tapestry weavers, sculptors and silversmiths.

The broad basis of an art-school education in the 1920s encouraged the growth of Spence's creative skills and instilled in him a sympathy for the contribution of other artists. With time allocated to architecture and painting equally balanced, Spence developed a rare facility for graphic representation – a dangerous talent in the eyes of later commentators. It was also at the College that his place within a Scottish architectural culture, rather than a British, was established. This was arguably to be a lasting influence on his work.

As a student, Spence flourished within the rarefied atmosphere of the College of Art. Elected secretary of the Students' Association in 1926, the young dapper Spence, with what a later commentator called *'an eye for women'*,[3] immersed himself in the liberating ambience of a college of art. If Spence enjoyed college life, he did not neglect his studies. Within a year he had been awarded a maintenance bursary on the basis of grades which record distinctions for design work[4]. Two years later Spence was again rewarded with high marks for studio projects, but low marks for building construction. The problem of understanding the technical aspects of building continued through his architectural training and, according to contemporaries, into his professional life. In his third year Spence was *'highly commended'* for his sketching and measuring of Gothic buildings.

Practical training in the office of Sir Edwin Lutyens

After four years of study, Spence was awarded the College Certificate in Architecture which carried an exemption from the Royal Institute of British Architects (RIBA) Intermediate Examination. He also left college with the Royal Incorporation of Architects in Scotland Prize, on the basis of his growing skill as an architectural draughtsman. With certificates, RIBA exemption and prizes obtained, Spence left Edinburgh for London in the summer of 1929 to work in the office of Sir Edwin Lutyens. Lutyens was then the pre-eminent architect in England and engaged on the prestigious building of the government offices at New Delhi. Spence was employed for a year as an assistant working, exclusively, on the Viceroy's House where his attentions were directed towards furniture and garden design. Besides New Delhi, Lutyens was engaged in the design of military cemeteries for the British and Australian Governments as well as a number of private houses. Spence would, therefore, have had much to see and discuss with colleagues. Christopher Hussey recalls that the exacting standards of Lutyens did not prevent him from being *'a kind, if stern, critic of young men's work'*.[5]

Spence later acknowledged that Lutyens was *'his patron and master'*[6] and that the year in the London office had influenced his approach to design. The monumental tendency visible in New Delhi and the skilful handling of solid and void in various war memorials impressed him – as did the Lutyens' office drawing style – with its dramatic shadows, shafts of light and grand processional stairways.

If something of the geometric monumentality of Lutyens'

NMRS (Ewing Collection)

Perspective drawing of St Salvator's Church, St Andrews, prepared in October 1929 while Spence was a student at Edinburgh College of Art.

Spence's early interest in medieval architecture, nurtured by a sketching tour of Yorkshire cathedrals in 1927 and French châteaux a year later, may have been an important influence on his later development. Not only was Spence to produce superb perspectives, infused with the spirit of Gothic, for architects such as L G Thomson; but as a designer for later buildings such as Coventry Cathedral, Spence was especially fascinated by questions of light, structure and interior space.

Besides working a full day in Lutyens' office, the young assistant enrolled for evening classes at the Bartlett School of Architecture. There he met Albert Richardson, Professor of Architecture, an accomplished scholar and inspiring teacher. With another Bartlett professor, Hector Corfiato, Richardson wrote *The Art of Architecture*, a book which had yet to appear when Spence was an evening-class student. But no doubt the lectures formed the basis of its material, which proposed that *'character in architecture is essentially a deductive quality, that is to say, it depends upon the power of the designer to express outwardly the arrangement he has planned within'.*[7] Ironically, Spence later found his design for Coventry Cathedral criticised by Richardson, then a member of the Royal Fine Art Commission.

designs influenced the young Spence, he may also have been impressed by the perspective style of William Walcot. Copies of the dozen fine perspectives of New Delhi and other lesser sketches of further projects prepared for Lutyens by Walcot sat in Lutyens' office when Spence was employed there in 1930. There is something of Walcot's dramatic perspective style and his apparently effortless handling of planes of watercolour in the paintings of Spence. Unlike other perspectivists of the period, Spence was to dispense with detail and concentrate rather more upon colour and atmosphere.

The return to Edinburgh

The inspiration of Lutyens and Albert Richardson helped Spence produce his best student work. On his return to Edinburgh in 1930 he was awarded top marks for design and the Rowand Anderson Silver Medal. A year later he won the RIBA Silver Medal as the best architectural student in the United Kingdom. In 1933 he was awarded the equally prestigious Pugin Student Prize for sketches and measured drawings of Gothic architecture. Jointly with Robert Matthew, he also won the Arthur Cates Prize for town planning, a reflection of his interest in place making rather than merely

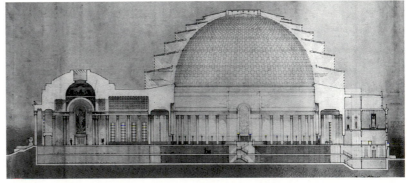

NMRS (Ewing Collection)

Design for a national library prepared as a submission for the Soane Medallion in 1931-2.

the design of buildings. Of the project work prepared by Spence at the College only a few examples survive – a design for a national library in London prepared for the Soane Medallion (see p.53) and a collection of freehand drawings such as that of the organ screen at St Salvator's Church, St Andrews. The former, of almost baroque proportions, consists of a huge circular reading room with light filtering diaphanously through a honeycomb of stepped windows in the drum. His enduring interest in light, space and internal architectural drama is captured better in this design than any work until the ICI Pavilion at the 1938 Empire Exhibition.

In October 1931 Spence joined the office of Rowand Anderson, Balfour Paul, after obtaining his diploma from Edinburgh College of Art in June of that year. His friend William Kininmonth, who had graduated a year earlier, had been offered an assistantship by Arthur Balfour Paul but had turned it down unless Basil Spence could come along too. Paul could not afford two assistants but, liking Spence, suggested the two could share a salary and a drawing board. Kininmonth was clearly of generous spirit for he agreed to splitting the fairly meagre salary of £12 per month. With only half their time committed to Rowand Anderson's office, Kininmonth and Spence formed their own partnership for the remainder. The practice of Kininmonth and Spence, though not formally constituted, undertook commissions independently of the office of Rowand Anderson, Balfour Paul. This loose alliance produced some of the city's more interesting early Modernist houses. At both the Braid Estate, where Anderson's office had overall responsibility as feuing architect, and in the Murrayfield area, the practice of Kininmonth and Spence engaged in building white, prismatic houses with cut-away corners and horizontal windows (see p.49). At the same time both Spence and Kininmonth taught part-time at Edinburgh College of Art.

During the year in Lutyens' office Spence met his future wife, Mary Joan Ferris, playing badminton at a London club.[8] She had recently moved from the West Country to stay with an aunt in Clapham in order to establish a secretarial career for herself. Coming from a large middle-class family, she found the young, urbane Spence, then a stranger to London, an attractive companion and subsequent correspondent on his return to Scotland. They married five years later.

Even after being made a partner in 1934, Spence had time to produce coloured chalk and pencil views for other architects' designs. In 1935 the Kirkcaldy practice of Williamson and Hubbard paid eight guineas for a *'perspective sketch'* and a year later the Edinburgh architect, W J Walker Todd, paid twenty-one guineas for two perspectives. Spence had also draughted perspectives for J Reginald Fairlie and Leslie Graham Thomson.

The office of Rowand Anderson, Balfour Paul became Rowand Anderson, Paul and Partners in 1934 when both Spence and Kininmonth were made partners. Surprisingly, the loose alliance of Kininmonth and Spence continued after they had been formally absorbed into the practice as junior partners. The office was under the guidance of John McClure Anderson who directed affairs on behalf of Balfour Paul. In addition, there was a chief draughtsman, three assistant draughtsmen and four apprentices.

Added to the flow of design work coming into the office of Rowand Anderson, Paul and Partners, the ledger books itemise perspective drawings prepared for other firms. The reputation of Spence as a perspective artist was such that his skills were required by others. The motivation for such work may have been the fees which could be earned: Spence was then earning £20 a month and a perspective drawing probably did not take longer than two days to prepare. With the firm sometimes only able to earn a fee of one and a half percent for designing buildings as large and complex as Quothquhan (the total fee at Quothquhan was a mere £106), perspectives were a worthwhile sideline. Another source of income was Spence's employment as a lecturer at Edinburgh College of Art. He, along with Kininmonth, taught architectural design to students, acting as a studio instructor rather than formal lecturer. His income of about £300 a year from the College exceeded his salary as a partner with Balfour Paul throughout much of the 1930s.

View of house at 6 Castlelaw Road, Colinton, showing debt to Lorimer's 'Colinton-style'.

Brian Edwards

The practice of Kininmonth and Spence and suburban houses

Despite their elevation to partners in 1934, Kininmonth and Spence continued to build work in the Edinburgh area on their own account until 1939. Almost exclusively modest houses, some may have been commissions considered too small for the Balfour Paul office to handle, and others came as a result of contacts of Kininmonth's brother, Gordon; as an Edinburgh radiologist he introduced doctor friends to the young practice. Because of the friendship between Kininmonth and Spence and their similar backgrounds, it is not easy to distinguish the authorship of early designs, although the draughtsmanship is quite distinctive. It is said that Spence was the designer and Kininmonth the constructor. But both men were talented designers who shared an architectural ambition to be able to design in a variety of styles. Kininmonth's own house at 46a Dick Place is a remarkably assured essay in white cubic architecture. Built in 1933, this small abstract composition of squares and semicircles beneath a flat roof and with open-plan interiors suggests that Kininmonth had a clear grasp of International Style principles. In contrast, the design Spence furnished the same year for his mother's house on the Braid Estate in Comiston Rise is more rooted in tradition. The legacy of Lorimer can be seen in the shaped gables, low slung roofs, white walls and circulation arranged around a long gallery on the north side. These Scottish features are lightened with touches of Modernist practice such as horizontally banded windows, semicircular arched doorways, and square-gridded oak front doors. Although extended after Spence's day, the Comiston Rise house was a modest, well-crafted bungalow for a mother who had returned to Scotland on the death of her husband a few months earlier. Since the early gas bills are in Basil Spence's own name, the house may also have been his early matrimonial home.

A common feature of these early houses is the inventive use of aspect and orientation. Many of the design drawings make prominent display of the north point, and there are often comments about angles for the best views. Sunshine, open aspect and prospect seem to have been the main generators of site and house planning. Spence invariably placed the

Perspective drawing by Spence of house at 6 Castlelaw Road, Colinton.

Brian Edwards

NMRS (Ewing Collection)

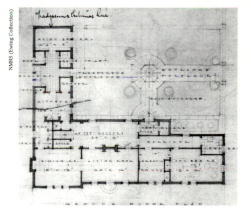

Design for a house at 6 Castlelaw Road, Colinton, prepared by Kininmonth and Spence in 1932 for Sir James Allan. This is the first design constructed for the young practice.

Below *Doorway detail at 220 Braid Road, Edinburgh.*
Bottom *View of house in Comiston Rise, Edinburgh, designed in 1936 by Spence for his mother.*

Brian Edwards

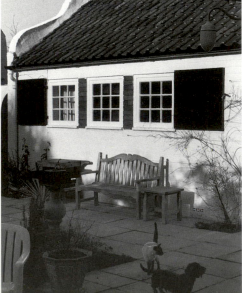

Brian Edwards

entrance on the north side, opening the living rooms to the south. At 57 Oxgangs Road, 1936, designed for James Duncan, Spence mixed an orthodox north elevation of almost Georgian simplicity with a highly glazed south elevation. Inside the house all is white and well proportioned. The entrance hall is almost a pure cube – its height, width and depth being close to nine feet. Doors are placed opposite each other and the stair rises elegantly to be lit by a tall sash window on the half landing. Arguably, it is the most refined, if traditional, of Spence's early suburban houses.

Between 1931 and 1939 Kininmonth and Spence designed at least six houses of Classical rather than Arts and Crafts inspiration. The group began with Glenburn House in Glenlockhart, Edinburgh, inspired perhaps by the sober and restrained Classicism of eighteenth-century Scottish houses, and ended with Quothquhan. Spence's neo-Georgian group of houses is carefully planned, well executed and displays an adept facility for disciplined geometric planning. Though he embraces the principles of Classicism, he often departs from its detailed vocabulary. Although one cannot attribute the neo-Georgian group of houses (except Quothquhan) to Spence alone, his hand can be detected perhaps in the formal arrangements and concern for volumetric contrasts.

An early Arts and Crafts house, possibly Spence's first villa design, is to be found at 6 Castlelaw Road, Colinton. Designed in July 1932 for Sir James Allan who owned a string of shoe shops in the city, the elevation of the house draws upon the Lorimer aesthetic, already well established in this suburb, of shaped gables, projecting wings and picturesque grouping, contrasting with a formal garden design. A galleried entrance hall runs along the north side of the house providing shelter from cold winds. Living accommodation spreads out to the south and west and connects with the garden via large sash windows and French doors. The expansive style, timber window shutters and sweeping roofs give the house a colonial air at times.

In typical Scots fashion, Spence reserved ornamentation for the places where it mattered, leaving other surfaces plain. His Arts and Crafts houses invariably had oak framed doorways, often with a grid of lights set in square frames. The dextrous handling of interior light, sunshine and volume contrast with traditional exterior elements on the outside such as exaggerated chimneys, pitched roofs and harled walls. Moreover, the juxtaposition of contrasting materials (tile, slate, render and stone) is used by Spence as an expressive, rather than formal, means of design.

In the conception of the design of the dozen or so early houses of Kininmonth and Spence there is a discernible struggle between an emphasis on the 1930s Arts and Crafts manner and an adoption of smooth planes and white abstraction of the International Style. The conflict is most noticeable in the collection of Murrayfield houses built around 1935 (seep.51, 53). At Lismhor, 11 Easter Belmont Road, for Dr John King, a horizontally disposed base of steps and retaining walls provide a well-buttressed platform on which to build a daring Modernist house. Kininmonth and Spence employed crisp white terraces and walls to resolve the compositional conflict between horizontal and vertical lines. Low-slung windows, which cut into the cube of the house at corners, and wide semicircular bow windows seem to echo the sweeping contours and help marry the building to the site. The smooth modernity of the house was the result of the client's taste as well as his architect's.

Dr King built the house for his wife who was suffering from tuberculosis. He insisted that every room faced south and that the house was thoroughly and conspicuously ventilated. As a result, 11 Easter Belmont Road has the air of a sanatorium with sunshine flooding onto the smooth, polished surfaces of every

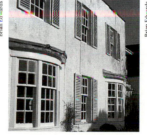

Above *House at 57 Oxgangs Road, Edinburgh, designed in 1935 by Kininmonth and Spence. The architects' admiration of Regency buildings is evident in this design.*
Right *Present view from garden of 11 Easter Belmont Road, Edinburgh.*

A recurrent theme in Kininmonth and Spence commissions is the use of round-arched openings picked out in decorative tilework. At 220 Braid Road, Spence used two courses of blue pantiles set on edge in white cement to define the entrance doorway and a similar detail is found around the main fireplace in Comiston Rise.

Kininmonth admitted that King was *'the only ideal client we ever had'.*[9] King had toured Germany and had seen first-hand the work of such architects as Peter Behrens, Walter Gropius and Max Taut.[10] He had visited the Werkbund Weissenhof Housing Exhibition in 1927 and was keen to bring progressive design ideas to the more conservative environment of Murrayfield.

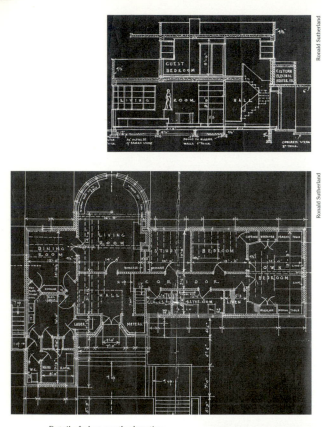

Ronald Sutherland

Detail of plan, north elevation and section of working drawing for Dr King's house at 11 Easter Belmont Road, Edinburgh, designed in 1935.

room. There is, in addition, a sleeping balcony placed high on the south elevation overlooking the garden. It is a perfect semicircle placed above the glazed demi-rotunda of the living room below, reminiscent of a similar arrangement in Kininmonth's own house in Dick Place.

The courtyard house at 4 Easter Belmont Road for Miss Reid repeats the same elements, though with less panache. The plan (not fully realised) is particularly interesting: a square courtyard set centrally within a square house. The sitting room projects out from the perimeter of the square with a semicircular bow window. All is carefully considered and suggests that Kininmonth and Spence were able to fuse a new order out of residential programmes. However, in spite of the gestures towards modernity, Scotland's climate still dictated a pitched roof. The handling of architectural mass and the balance between horizontal and vertical lines give these houses the air of formal experiments. Though the architects adopted the idiom of the International Style at a decorative level, the architecture of these houses remained traditional in construction which circumvented the adoption of an interior free plan.

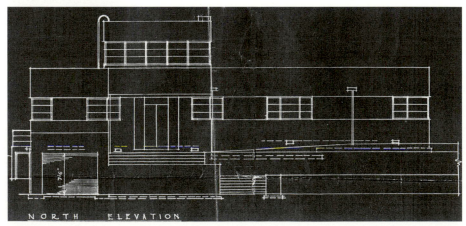

NORTH ELEVATION

Ronald Sutherland

A trio of mansions: Broughton Place, Quothquhan and Gribloch

After 1936 the practice Rowand Anderson, Paul and Partners won a number of commissions for houses of real substance, three of which deserve particular attention: Broughton Place, near Tweedsmuir, Quothquhan near Biggar and Gribloch near Kippen, north of Glasgow. All three country houses in their own estate presented the architects with a challenge – to reconcile views, sunshine and practical arrangements. The trio is attributed mainly to Spence, though each is remarkably different in form, style and detail.

Broughton Place was the first of this important trio. It was built in 1936 on a hillside a few miles south of Biggar for Professor Thomas and Lady Elliott who, instead of buying an old house, decided to build one instead. The house is an assured essay in Scottish Renaissance architecture, beautifully crafted in cavity brickwork with a white render and the occasional carved stone panel by the sculptor Hew Lorimer, all beneath a fine slate roof. Spence had the pleasant job of creating a country estate complete with cottages, stables and a doocot. Broughton Place is a stylish twentieth-century Scots Revival house and demonstrates the breadth of Spence's ambitions as an architect at the time.

Broughton Place adopts the familiar Spence arrangement of an access road placed on the north side with living rooms extending outwards to the south and overlooking a formal garden. A raised terrace to the north set in the shallow angle between the service wing and turreted staircase provides access to a centrally placed front door. Internally, Spence expands upon the arrangement of his earlier houses with a grand entrance gallery, decorated here with Renaissance flourishes and extending for the full depth of the building. The design is an essay in what has been called the 'third Scottish Revival' and exploits seventeenth-century principles of house planning with its large, well-proportioned rooms

His task at Broughton Place was, no doubt, helped by having re-cased Liberton House near Edinburgh a year earlier: a harled L-plan house, originally built in 1600, which Spence was instrumental in restoring to its original form.

Top *Detail of carved panel by Hew Lorimer at Broughton Place.*
Above *View of Broughton Place in 1954.*

The ability of Spence to design in this fashion, while, in contrast, creating proto-modern buildings of the calibre of Causewayside garage in Edinburgh, shows he could exploit fully two principal themes of Scottish architecture – tradition and modernity.

At the time, Erskine-Hill was the MP for North Edinburgh; later, as Chairman of the influential 1922 Committee, he damaged his career by opposing Churchill. He was clearly a client who knew his mind and Spence deferred to his judgement regarding architectural taste.

An earlier design by Spence, with a view of the house framed by pines, was greatly altered at the instruction of the Erskine-Hills. A square porch, designed by Spence to read as a small cube placed in front of a large one, was abandoned, and the service wing was moved from the east to the west side, presumably to act as a windbreak.

and massive fireplaces. Three years later he referred to the importance of the *'judicious selection of forms'* from the Renaissance, arguing that they adapted well to modern conditions.[11]

Quothquhan is a less competent essay in historicism, this time of eighteenth-century Scottish Classicism. Culter House, near Biggar, a white Scottish house of Georgian purity built in the early eighteenth century, provided the inspiration. Spence was taken here in 1937 by Quothquhan's client Mrs Erskine-Hill as an example of what to build. Mr and Mrs Alexander G Erskine-Hill (later knighted) sought a country house to use for holidays and weekends. Having rented Culter a few years earlier, they regarded it as a model of Scottish rural perfection.

The chosen site for Quothquhan was part of the ancient estate of Libberton in Lanarkshire, on the wide flood plain of the upper Clyde. Here, fertile fields in the troughs of valleys merge into the broad plantations of Scots Pine which encircle the lower slopes of upland hills. One such plantation of pines and firs was sufficiently large to absorb the country house and yet not extensive enough to block views across the Clyde to distant hills.

Perspective drawing by Spence of main elevation to Quothquhan, Lanarkshire, prepared in 1936.

Having visited Culter with Mrs Erskine-Hill, Spence knew what was expected. His design of a three-bay, two-storey house, linked via splayed service wings and garage block with the surrounding landscape, repeats Culter in its general form. Invention with such clients was reserved for site planning, and here Spence excelled. The winding drive through the dark forest suddenly opens onto a white house of geometric purity. The formality, reinforced by Classical proportions, is further underlined by the modulation of the house into a central block with wings which advance at the ends. The iconographic language is undeniably of the early eighteenth century, yet the finer touches suggest a modern sensibility. Quothquhan was described by Spence as *'the happiest house he ever built'*.[12]

As usual with Spence, the entrance was placed to the north with a gallery providing access to public rooms arranged on the south. At Quothquhan a raised terrace to the rear is set between two projecting wings which provide shelter from the Lanarkshire winds. This terrace faces a splayed viewing slot cut through the forest which focuses on Tinto Hill in the distance. Just as at Broughton, Spence orchestrates landscape and building design to bring nature and sunshine to the steps of the house. The care Spence took to allow sunshine to penetrate his houses in general, and Quothquhan in particular, means that his south and north elevations appear quite distinctive. At Quothquhan the north front is treated in a scenic fashion – it is wide and embracing with a welcoming air – but the south is open, penetrable by light and united via terraces with the vast landscape in which it sits.

The final house in Spence's trio of large Scottish residences is Gribloch, built for the steel magnate John Colville just outside Kippen. It too is set deeply into the countryside and provided Spence with a challenge – to reconcile a bracing, open view with sunshine and shelter. At Gribloch, Spence had the task of satisfying a modern Scottish industrialist and his

Brian Edwards

View of Quothquhan today: main elevation.

The interiors of Quothquhan are noticeably plain employing unity, control and restrained décor for effect. Simple panel doors and large sash windows in Oregon Pine provide the only references to Georgian precedents. It is as if Spence saw the Classical language as an external affair, preferring instead to use light and space as the main elements for internal expression.

It was a plan arrived at after much graphic experimentation. At Gribloch the path of the sun and direction of view, considered one of the finest in Scotland, were in roughly opposite directions, and Spence selected an eastern approach with the main accommodation arranged in two angled wings orientated towards the west.

The office ledger books allude to the difficulties experienced by Spence as he sought to move from broad to detailed design. Reference is made to submitting *'further schemes'*, of *'discussing various further points'*, or of *'sending drawings of the latest scheme of the home'*.[13]

American wife. Their different tastes proved a source of difficulty for the architect. Spence was required, at various times, to collaborate with American and French 'consultants', including the New York architect Perry Duncan.[14]

Spence began designing Gribloch early in 1937 though the house was not occupied until late in 1939. For the first year Spence and Colville appear to have developed the design in a harmonious relationship. Though Colville was an exacting client with definite views of his own regarding house design, Spence had evolved a broad concept in the first few weeks with, unusually, the entrance and driveway facing east, thereby allowing the living accommodation to spread outwards towards both view and afternoon sun via splayed wings.

By mid-1938 Colville and Spence had a working plan. The entrance hall facing east led to a handsome stairway set against a glazed semicircular bow window. The influence of Gropius and Mendelsohn is evident (both had recently lectured at Edinburgh College of Art) and captured more vividly in the design sketches by Spence than in the final building. The glazed elliptical stair, subsequently flattened to a shallow bow, became the main generator of the plan and termination to a grand spacious hall. Two angled wings set approximately forty degrees apart frame a formal pool (initially conceived as a swimming pool) which extends beyond the house into the wider landscape. To the north a bold curved window opens from the spacious interior onto a view of Ben Lomond (delightfully captured in a Spence perspective drawing) while the southern wing is reserved for service accommodation.

The use of shallow angled wings, glazed rounded corners, a central sunlit hall with Hollywood-Regency decoration (see p.50) and nearly flat roofs set Gribloch apart from Spence's other large houses. If Broughton and Quothquhan are traditional houses tempered by a little modernity, Gribloch is

Three development sketches by Spence of different planning arrangements for Gribloch analysed
against view, sunshine, access and composition. These sketches accompanied letters to the Colvilles in 1938.

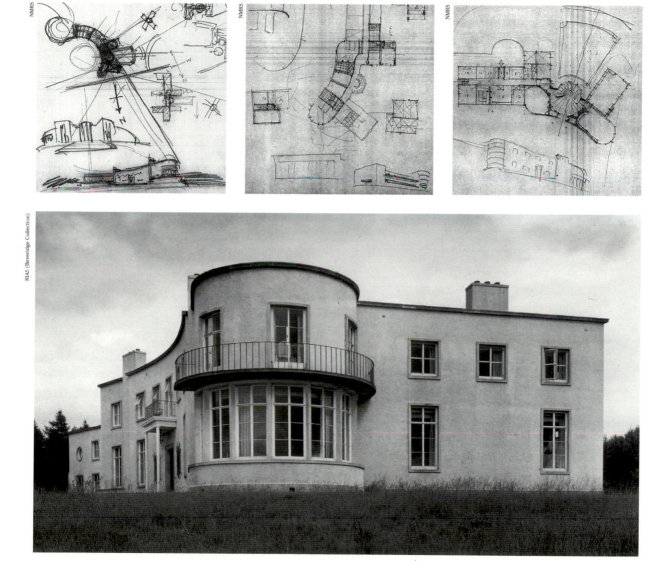

View of Gribloch in the 1940s: entrance elevation.

a modern house tempered by a little tradition. Random details allude to Scottish building practice, such as raised window margins and stone trim, but the general massing and bold arrangement of the design sets the house clearly within the progressive style of 1930s architecture.

If Quothquhan was a happy house for Spence, Gribloch was less so. An increasingly disgruntled client (incidentally a cousin of Alexander Erskine-Hill) who sought the opinion of other designers on Spence's work. Various overseas architects were consulted, most notably the American Perry Duncan who appears to have offered advice mainly on the interiors. The art historian Nikolaus Pevsner, already well known through articles in *Architectural Review*, was also consulted on the design of the entrance hall, no doubt adding to the strain between client and architect. The difficulties presented by husband and wife, who sought two quite different houses and who often disagreed about the design, may have been a strain too great in the end for Spence. The divergent ambitions of the three were never fully resolved and the house, completed without the style of the earlier sketches, was described by one perceptive visitor as *'rather like an overworked watercolour'*.[15]

The three large country houses suggest that Spence was flexible in his application of Modernist doctrine. Spence and Kininmonth were proud to be able to change their designs to suit the taste of their clients. An essentially Humanist quality sets Spence apart from more authoritarian contemporaries. It was a quality acknowledged by *The Times* which said in its obituary to Spence that his freedom from ideals and willingness to put pictorial conception before design dogma made him a *'man of the eighteenth rather than twentieth century'*.[16] At Gribloch the marriage of modern principles of house planning with traditional methods of construction resulted in a house which never appealed to avant-garde

View of Gribloch in the 1940s: garden front.

RIAS (Beveridge Collection)

critics. Consequently, Gribloch has been overlooked by historians of twentieth-century architecture despite its rational plan and skilful exploitation of sunshine and view.

Garages, department stores and exhibition designs: 1930-40

For inter-war Britain, the growth in car ownership created a market for roadside hotels and service stations. In 1933 Spence was given the commission to design the Causewayside garage in Edinburgh (see p.56). He avoided

Spence records that, although Le Corbusier's *Towards a New Architecture* was considered subversive literature in Lutyens' office, he was greatly influenced by its contemporary philosophy: Southern Motors provided Spence with his first commercial client in sympathy with its ideals.

NMRS (Ewing Collection)

Perspective drawing by Spence of garage for Southern Motors at Causewayside, Edinburgh, designed by Kininmonth and Spence in 1933.

fashionable Art Deco detail, using instead a disciplined play of solid and transparent elements, balancing horizontal and vertical planes. The resulting design, captured admirably in perspectives by Spence, displays a sound grasp of International Style principles.

Here the architect adopts a free plan, an expressive, independent structure with glazing which spreads in standardised pattern across the street elevation. Where earlier, Spence had created the effect of mass and solidity, here the feeling for volume and smooth white surfaces is dominant. With the inclusion of a circular office suite behind the petrol pumps, there is a hint of Le Corbusier's influence, particularly the phase known as 'purism'. The inclusion of the curved form within the rectilinear profile of the garage and the daringly expressed cantilever are surely precursors of the post-war designs of Basil Spence.

Besides the design of the garage at Causewayside, Spence's main commercial work was for department stores in Edinburgh and Glasgow. Cleghorn's in George Street, Edinburgh, was a design of 1937 attributed jointly to Kininmonth and Spence. Occupying a corner position, the shop exploited transparency to good effect. A large plate-glass window set in minimal steel frames allowed pavement shoppers to peer directly into the store. The architectural frame of the shopfront embraced a panel for the Cleghorn sign and, once inside, the simple rectangle of interior space was dominated by circular light wells cut into the ceiling. These not only allowed light to filter down from above but introduced a favourite Spence motif of circles within a square. Another Spence trick (developed at Gribloch) is to be seen in the circular staircase rising along a wall with its presence marked here by a red cylinder (see p.52).

Exhibition designs before the war

The third important strand of work for Spence in the 1930s concerned the design of exhibition stands and pavilions. This rather specialist field began in 1936 when office records refer to Spence preparing designs for the Scottish pavilion at the Johannesburg Exhibition in South Africa. He also carried out lesser designs for the Edinburgh Architectural Association stand at Waverley Market and an exhibition for the Royal Scottish Museum. No clue is given in contemporary accounts as to why the relatively inexperienced Spence was given these important commissions. Perhaps his fluent drawing style and general flamboyance appealed to the Scottish Development Council which was his prime client. These early forays into exhibition design provided Spence with an opportunity to travel and a chance to experiment with new lightweight materials. Office letters and account books refer to Spence visiting factories to inspect materials and to liaise with manufacturers of stands. Compared to the more basic technology of his housing and commercial buildings, this work held the promise of a truly contemporary architecture where light, space, frame and panel could be separately expressed.

The first allusion to Spence's involvement in the Empire Exhibition occurred in August 1936 when he was invited to a meeting in Glasgow of the Scottish Development Council.[17] Soon after, on 7 October 1936, Spence met the person responsible for the overall design of the exhibition, Thomas Tait, to 'take instructions'. Tait was then the most prominent and respected Scots architect of the inter-war period. He had just completed the design of government offices at St Andrew's House, Edinburgh. Tait had the task of producing the layout plan, of advising on the appointment of designers for individual pavilions and overseeing costs estimated at £11.5 million.[18] Although Tait had overall control and supported young designers with progressive views, the main industrial

ICI pavilion at the Empire Exhibition designed by Spence.

The design of exhibitions was also well paid – an important consideration for an architect about to become a father; his fee of £105 in 1936 for the Scottish pavilion at the Johannesburg Exhibition was almost exactly the same as that for Quothquhan.

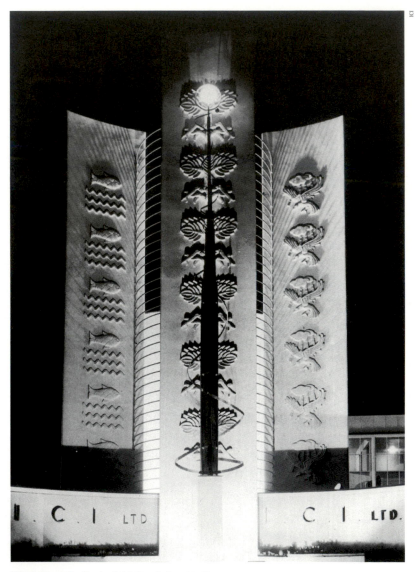

ICI pavilion at the Empire Exhibition designed by Spence.

exhibitors could employ their own architects. So we find Spence simultaneously taking instructions from Tait to enable him to design the Council for Art and Industry pavilion and from ICI for their pavilion. Quite how Spence secured his place on the list of four architects invited to submit designs for the prestigious ICI pavilion remains a mystery. Perhaps Tait had recommended Spence or alternatively ICI had been impressed by the stands at the Johannesburg Exhibition and the Royal Scottish Museum. Certainly ICI required a designer to set their products in a pavilion of contemporary spirit and Spence had already demonstrated his facility for working with new lightweight materials and structures.

By June 1937 Spence was well into the process of designing the ICI pavilion, having won the limited competition. His time was greatly taken up with visits to London to discuss his plans directly with senior staff at ICI headquarters. The brief to Spence was the creation of a pavilion which appealed to the layman by firing his imagination with the importance of the chemical industry.[19] ICI saw the Empire Exhibition not as a Scottish event but as one of wider importance where the pavilion was to stress the international character of the company with its links throughout the Empire. Because of the relatively small site (80ft x 50ft) Spence was instructed not to create individual exhibits but a pavilion whose design, decoration and actual construction, embodied within a tower, represented the character and manufacturing interests of ICI.

For Spence, hitherto mainly engaged upon the design of Scottish houses for conservative clients, the brief from ICI offered fresh opportunities. He designed the pavilion as a unified conception without compartments and the clutter of commercial products. Those at ICI who briefed Spence wisely felt that, if specific products were on display, the pavilion would end up looking like *'a cross between a chemist's store and a junk-shop'*.[20] Instead, ICI was keen that the pavilion be built

The Tree and the Worm – an emblem of Earth, designed by Mr T Whalen, on one of the three pylons of the pavilion of Imperial Chemical Industries (ICI).

Spence, now thirty years old, impressed the architect Robert Hurd who described the ICI pavilion as the best exhibit of the Empire Exhibition. [21]

His interest in formal rather than structural systems is evident in the lack of visible construction; Spence arranged the parts in the style of a fine artist rather than an engineer.

of its own synthetic materials, and Spence had the task of employing ICI's modern chemical finishes, non-ferrous metals and dyes in an architectural context.

Spence's conception consisted of three pylons representing the raw materials of the chemical industry – Earth, Air and Water – set against a beam of light depicting the fourth element, Fire. The tall rectangular pylons, each decorated in motifs to represent their subject, were braced by curved cupronickel tubes which set line against plane. Beyond the entrance pylon, a glass-roofed rotunda provided the focus for ICI exhibits. In these ways Spence employed circle and cube, line and abstract decoration, in a contemporary fashion.

Writing much later, Spence acknowledged the support and encouragement he received from Thomas Tait, recounting that the organising architect was *'very complimentary'* about the ICI pavilion.[22]

The other pavilions designed by Spence at the Empire Exhibition provided no less opportunity for the architect to display his grasp of modern design principles. The hovering volumes and weightless illusion of the Scottish pavilion, designed by Spence, draw directly from progressive European practice. The Spence sketch of the Scottish Pavilion shows an assembly of horizontally disposed blocks held together by a central, cut-away tower. The smooth, clean geometric shapes with banded windows and expressive entrance porch, are a development of ideas found earlier in the architect's work – his house for Dr King for example. While the ICI pavilion was curvilinear, that representing Scottish nationhood was straight, strict and formal. The austerity of the planes of its wall and glass-prismed tower was offset by superimposed images of the Scottish lion. As at ICI a lingering taste for decorative ornament marks Spence's architecture at this time. His architecture, though formally in advance of many of his contemporaries, provided wallspace for artists and sculptors.

Scottish pavilion at the Empire Exhibition, 1938.

Mitchell Library, Glasgow

A curved apse-like room in the Scottish pavilion, glazed within a square grid of pine, created a well-lit setting for figurative sculpture by Archibald Dawson.

The task of exhibition designers is to create eyecatching belvederes or enclosures. Here, according to Spence, the architect has to be something of a showman employing *'spirited, light, gay and cohesive architecture'* to prevent exhibitions becoming tiring places.[23] The ICI and Scottish pavilions display a freedom of design so far hidden from view in Spence's work. He shows a willingness to combine an essentially Scottish interest in strong geometry, powerful rhythms and dramatic light with the more subtle demands of lightweight framing, prefabrication and modern synthetic materials. Writing in 1950 Spence acknowledged that exhibitions were *'fundamentally the forcing house for experiment which would take on more solid form at some later date'.*[24]

Early council housing in pre-war Scotland

There was another strand in Spence's widening portfolio of work in the 1930s which concerned the design of council housing for a number of Scottish authorities. The report of the Royal Commission of 1917 into working-class housing in Scotland recommended that powers be given to town councils to enable them to build houses to offset the shortfall in demand provided by private landlords. The Royal Commission's recommendations were subsequently incorporated into the Scottish Housing Acts of 1923, 1924, 1930 and 1935. For architects in private practice these acts introduced a useful and growing source of employment in the pre-war years. Rowand Anderson, Paul and Partners benefited particularly from this new area of work. By being well known in country areas for their private houses and restorations, it was in the small towns rather than cities that Spence was to leave his mark.

The ability of Spence to create avant-garde architecture and to provide the setting for contemporary artists made him a suitable architect for the design of exhibition pavilions. This creative generosity found expression much later in the design for the British Pavilion Expo '67 where Spence deliberately engineered space and light to set the artistic exhibits of Tess Jaray to best advantage.

Brian Edwards

Above *Council housing by the sea in Dunbar.*
Opposite *Aerial perspective of Dunbar prepared in 1952 incorporating groups of houses designed by the practice from 1933 onwards.*

The Forth housing scheme, influenced by contemporary Swedish design, was painted in various shades of blue and quickly screened behind trees on the instructions of the client, the Scottish Special Housing Association, which found the buildings too bold for its taste.[25]

His wonderful perspective drawing of 1952 of housing at Dunbar, rendered at the level of a soaring seagull, shows both phases of the development. The sheds for fishermen's nets, the area for drying clothes and the quayside space for unloading boats are all considered and delineated as if as important as the buildings themselves.

The Royal Commission's report had a profound effect on the type of accommodation which was to be provided. The Commission was against the building of tenement blocks, blaming such schemes for Scotland's inheritance of poor housing and overcrowding; it preferred English-style terraces, 'four-in-a-block' cottages and, where tenements were unavoidable, these were to be only three storeys high and built with open ends for cross ventilation. Estates were preferably to be in garden suburbs with private gardens and plenty of open space. The influence of the English architect and town planner, Raymond Unwin, is to be found in much Scottish housing policy.

This background helps to explain the climate of opinion which existed when Spence was engaged on housing projects at Dunbar, Duns, Burnmouth, Forth and Selkirk just before and after the Second World War. In these schemes his designs are conservative by the standards of Europe; however, they show an approach to architecture which was particularly conscious of place. There is a willingness to create housing in formal courtyard groups rather than along estate roads and a fondness for traditional enclosed forms. His approach was not to abstract commissions into repetitive units but to build with a sense of locality and a regional identity. Even when he was appointed (with Kininmonth) to design 120 houses at Forth using what was then innovative timber-framed construction, his shallow-pitched roofed dwellings were grouped around courtyards each of which had a measure of urbanity.

Spence's prime concern as a designer of social housing seemed to be the creation of sunny quads, and this was achieved by the skilful grouping of terraces of houses and flats, ensuring that the new blended with the old.

Spence at Dunbar

In 1933 Kininmonth and Spence were appointed by the Burgh of Dunbar to prepare a town planning scheme for the harbour area. Large areas of unfit property were to be cleared under the Housing (Scotland) Act of 1930 and 38 houses built for local people, mainly fishermen's families.[26] Unfortunately for the young architects, the burgh council temporarily suspended the full scheme, arguing it was too extensive in area and too ambitious in scope. A year later, Kininmonth and Spence were asked to reconstruct their proposals for a section of the scheme, in the Victoria Street area, where ten houses were to be built at a cost of £3,500.

The design of the houses step down Victoria Street towards the harbour. Rather than follow the angle of the road, they form a right-angle with older neighbours thereby creating a square of space without delineated gardens, in front of the Victoria Arms Hotel. Each pair of houses is individually arranged but simultaneously united by a wide arch outlined in black tiles which embraces both front doors. The planes of white-painted brick wall sit on a base of red sandstone which not only picks up the line of ground-floor window cills, but also draws the eye to the older cottages and warehouses in the area. Spence deliberately mixes local materials with modern ones, such as metal-framed picture windows, not merely as picturesque streetscape, but intentionally to create visual continuity.

The terrace is formally restrained, suggestive of a bigger building. It is far less eclectic than Spence's later houses of 1953 which extend the development down to the quays. The later work is pretty as townscape, draws heavily upon a regional pattern of building and makes attractive courtyards of space. It is also Spence's most visible essay in combining the vernacular seaside revival with organic European stylistic forms.

The development when completed in 1954 won a Saltire Award and was widely referred to as an exemplar of urban conservation. One feels that the imagination and sparkle of Spence was restrained in the post-war development at Dunbar, his creativity clipped by a growing respect for preservation.

Aerial perspective by Spence of the entrance to the Scottish Industries Exhibition at Kelvin Hall held in 1949.

In the summer of 1945 Spence returned home from his duties, variously described as a staff captain and as a major in the British Army. He had spent the war years working as a camouflage officer, mainly seconded to the Camouflage Unit at Farnham in Hampshire and as an intelligence officer in Normandy where he was mentioned in two dispatches. In France he witnessed the destruction of beautiful Norman churches at Oustreham and Hermanville and, while sheltering in the trenches, proclaimed an ambition to build a cathedral. His return to the office of Rowand Anderson, Paul and Partners was not a happy one. Many projected schemes had been cancelled. The steady flow of work which marked the 1930s had given way to post-war austerity and a virtual moratorium on building construction. On his return to Rutland Square, still dressed in uniform, Spence was met, not by a flood of new commissions, but by a number of outstanding bills.[1] These were lean days for the construction industry in Scotland and Spence appears to have occupied his time with small commissions, such as the restoration and extension of a cottage in the Dean Village for the sculptor Alexander Zyw. Spence also resumed part-time teaching at Edinburgh College of Art. With little work in the offing he applied, in 1946, for membership of the RIBA. His application was supported by F R S Yorke and T S Tait.

Post-war exhibitions

In 1946 Spence and Bruce Robertson of Rowand Anderson's office formally constituted Basil Spence and Partners. A year later they employed Hardie Glover as an assistant, who became a partner in 1948. Spence had met Glover at the exhibition stand of Scandinavian furniture designed by the latter at the Wylie and Lochhead department store in Glasgow. Spence, an admirer of Scandinavian design, had been impressed by Glover's design and decided to travel back to Edinburgh with him.[2] Both men were much occupied with the

The design of exhibitions helped Spence pay for setting up his own practice on the ground floor of 40 Moray Place, Edinburgh. He, his wife Joan and their two small children Milton and Gillian, occupied a flat on the second floor. Although Spence was mainly active in exhibition architecture in Edinburgh and Glasgow, his talents were beginning to be recognised in London where touring displays from Scotland carried the distinctive stamp of the Spence exhibition style.

Airways stand designed by Spence at the Scottish Industries Exhibition, 1949.

RIAS

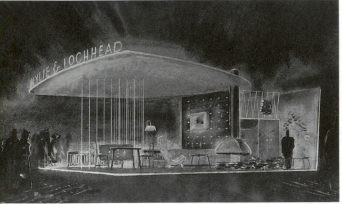

RIAS

Top *Scottish Industries Exhibition: J & P Coats Ltd pavilion.*
Above *Wylie & Lochhead pavilion.*

design of exhibition stands: Spence at the 'Enterprise Scotland' Exhibition in Edinburgh and the 'Britain Can Make It' Exhibition in London (where he was the co-ordinating architect), and Glover of trade exhibits in department stores. The journey by train from Glasgow to Edinburgh turned into something of a job interview and by their return to the capital Spence had offered Glover a job in his new practice.

Spence was both the overall designer of the Scottish Industries Exhibition held at Kelvin Hall in 1949 and architect for several of the individual stands. His approach was bold and colourful. Inside the hall he created a central avenue lined by pylons twenty feet high which marked the individual stands. Each pylon was festooned with banners based upon what Spence called *'a harmony of colour'*.[3] He selected eight complementary colours for the stands and set these against *'yards of material in striking shades of blue and yellow'*.[4] Spence used his position as co-ordinating architect to introduce colour and pattern, in contrast to the mainly white, smooth lines of the 1938 Glasgow Empire Exhibition. He also had the idea of enlivening the street frontage of the rather dated Kelvin Hall by adding a crescent of flagpoles to act as a screen to the dominating presence of Kelvingrove Art Gallery.

Five stands are worthy of attention, namely those for the Scottish Council of Industry, British Aluminium Company, ICI, Morris of Glasgow and the Airways stand for BEA, BOAC and BSAA. The Scottish Council of Industry stand consisted of a play of primary shapes – rotunda, pyramid, concave screen and dramatic angled pylon. Cables spread diagonally across the stand to hold the pylon in its angled position of sixty degrees. The arrowhead at the top of the pylon proclaiming 'design' reminded visitors of the Scottish Council of Industry's central concern for quality of design in Scottish products. A similar play of linear and curved elements made up the British Aluminium Company stand in which an aluminium sheet was

Scottish Industries Exhibition: ICI pavilion, as designed by Spence, displaying the lightness, openness and modernity of his architectural ambition after the war.

Morris had specified a laminated Canadian birchwood previously used in the construction of helicopter blades for the furniture. The suite had the elegant, almost Regency, air of bentwood furniture, with the addition of the distinctive elliptical graining of laminated timber. The graceful lines and subtlety of construction were of sufficient merit for a sample of the chairs to be acquired by the Museum of Modern Art in New York in 1960.

bent into a parabola to form an archway into the stand. Constructivist struts and angled supports criss-crossed the roof of the stand at various levels. An aluminium-hulled ship at the centre of the stand provided a focus for the bold geometries and freely expressed curves. Writing a year later about exhibition design Spence admitted that *'adventures into engineering theory . . . often supply the best possible effects'.*[5]

The ICI stand consisted of a double-height glass cube raised on a plinth and interpenetrated by a solid corner shaft used for the main displays. The balance between transparent and opaque elements is typical of Spence. Yet without the introduction of curves which provided the drama at the Spence-designed ICI pavilions elsewhere, the Kelvin Hall stand exploits for its main effect the play of panels and lines. At the stand for the furniture maker, Morris of Glasgow, Spence mixed screens and suspended planes at floor and roof level in a fashion reminiscent of Mies van der Rohe's Barcelona pavilion of 1936. At the same time Spence was asked by Morris' to design a suite of dining-room furniture in laminated timber. So the stand provided a shop window for the architect's first commercial designs for tables and chairs which were set in the pavilion against an abstract mural designed by Graham Sutherland.

The Airways pavilion for BEA, BOAC and BSAA shared features with the British Aluminium Company stand. It was formed from angled struts, cable-held roofs and curved displays. Raised above the ground suggesting the ascent into an aircraft, the cabins were designed to resemble a section cut through an aircraft fuselage.

These exhibition stands were direct precursors for the four pavilions designed by Spence for the Festival of Britain held two years later in London. What he had done at Kelvin Hall and Olympia proved equally applicable to the site overlooking the Thames on the South Bank. The Sea and Ships pavilion with its ship-like main hall and free-standing displays, based upon circles, inclined pylons and screen walls, evokes, on a grander scale, a combination of elements from his earlier stands. The Skylark Restaurant, Nelson Pier and Heavy Industries Exhibition develop concepts tested first in Glasgow, Edinburgh and to a lesser extent at the 'Britain Can Make It' Exhibition at Olympia.

Although the commission to design the pavilions came when Spence was still living in Scotland, by the time the Festival of Britain opened in May 1951, he had moved to London working out of an office in Canonbury, living, as in Edinburgh, above the drawing office. From there he was able to supervise the construction of his four pavilions. The development of the designs from early concept sketches by Spence was undertaken by staff in Moray Place, not London.[6] Thus these exciting structures are evidence of work matured in Scotland, simply supervised under construction from Canonbury. They represent the full flowering of the Spence imagination applied to temporary exhibition structures. The

Perspective drawing by Spence, 1949, of Sea and Ships pavilion at the Festival of Britain. Note the free expression of structure and the architect's exploitation of Constructivist vocabulary.

The clear influence of formal Constructivist arrangement allowed the artist in Spence to balance line against plane, and put bright colour alongside walls of white and steely grey. The deliberate disjointedness of the parts, particularly evident in the Sea and Ships pavilion, hints towards deconstruction. It was the last major opportunity Spence had to experiment within the specialised constraints of exhibition architecture.

Sea and Ships pavilion at the Festival of Britain, 1951.

RIAS

Above *Laminated plywood chair designed by Spence for Morris of Glasgow in 1949 using aircraft materials technology.*
Below *Boardroom table and chairs designed in 1951 by Spence displayed here at the Furniture Development Council Chamber, London.*

RIAS

Heavy Industries Exhibition and the Sea and Ships pavilion furthered the exploration of tensile cable-held structures, inclined pylons and thin membranes.

Work at Glasgow University

Two other major commissions stand out from a number of lesser works in the 1940s: the design of the Natural Philosophy building at Glasgow University and a large council-housing project at Bannerfield in Selkirk. Both date initially from 1947. The first was the result of the favourable impression left by the design of the exhibition at Kelvin Hall. The second was owing to the reputation Spence had achieved in his council housing from the 1930s.

Three architects were shortlisted and interviewed by Glasgow University – Jack Coia, Basil Spence and Professor Ronald Ward.[7] The University was in receipt of a grant from the Department of Science and Industry to build a synchrotron capable of producing an electronic charge of 200 million volts. There were important questions of radiation and structural stability to consider. As the University Court reported *'in such complicated buildings . . . the personality of the architect is of great importance . . . Mr Basil Spence seemed to us to be a very live wire and likely to make an original and rational approach to our problem'.*[8] Mr Coia was thought unlikely to get on well with research establishments and Ward, Slade Professor of Architecture at London University, was considered *'agreeable . . . but less energetic and less original than Mr Basil Spence'.*[9] Early in 1947 Spence was, therefore, given the commission to design one of the most demanding new buildings in post-war Britain. He faced two particular difficulties: the budget of £69,000 was barely sufficient for the task and the building had few precedents.

GLASGOW

Suite of dining-room chairs, table and sideboard designed by Spence for Morris of Glasgow seen here in front of the mural designed by Graham Sutherland at the exhibition stand at the Scottish Industries Exhibition.

RIAS

First phase of Natural Philosophy building at Glasgow University in 1952. Note how the smooth white planes contrast with the sensuality of natural materials surrounding the entrance.

NMRS (Ewing Collection)

NMRS (Ewing Collection)

Top *Unidentified house design of c.1934 by Kininmonth and Spence, probably for the Braid Estate. Notice the powerfully expressed chimney to balance the horizontal lines of windows: a common feature of later work.*
Above *Unspecified interior perspective of church showing Spence's recurring interest in angled light.*

Top and above *Two perspective views of Cleghorn's department store in George Street, Edinburgh, constructed in 1937. Note Spence's enduring interest in primary geometries, particularly the play of circles, squares and rectangles.*

Top *4 Easter Belmont Road, Edinburgh, designed by Kininmonth and Spence, 1935.*
Above *Spence student drawing of 1931 for a national library in London facing the*
Thames.

Brian Edwards

Household Cavalry Barracks, Knightsbridge, overlooking Hyde Park, London, 1970.

Brian Edwards

Edinburgh University Library, 1967. Powerful structural rhythms give the building great presence.

Southern Motors, Causewayside, Edinburgh. Spence perspective of 1933. Notice how the exaggerated cantilever breaks the smooth plane of glazing and the line of the flat roof.

The building responds pragmatically to its programme, the particle accelerator (the first erected in Scotland) expressed symbolically by way of a rotunda projecting through the roof of the north block. Spence, expressing structural rhythm and internal function in a frank fashion, employed a simple combination of Portland stone cladding, sandstone base, concrete and glass. There is little concession to either James Miller's neo-Jacobean building which formed an immediate neighbour or to the smooth, planar abstractions of the International Style.

The entrance is a generous sweep of steps, part cantilevered, leading to a well-lit hall and exhibition area protruding out at the angle between the west and north wings. The fenestration too is largely in accordance with Modernist doctrine. Bands of windows placed horizontally contrast with windows framed in concrete which project imperceptibly forward from the Portland stone cladding. The opportunity for architectural expression would doubtless have been greater had Spence not (for safety reasons) to place the particle accelerator underground and insulate it behind a 150 ton sliding door.

Perspective drawing by Spence of the Natural Philosophy building at Glasgow University dated March 1947.

Bannerfield estate, Selkirk

The planning and detailed design of an estate of over 300 houses at the Bannerfield estate at Selkirk provided Spence with his second major building commission of the post-war decade. His client, the Royal Burgh of Selkirk, sought to take advantage of the powers of development provided under the Town & Country Planning Act of 1947. In the plans prepared in 1948 (the year he was awarded the OBE) Spence abandoned picturesque tendencies evident at Dunbar and followed rational planning principles. His layout is strictly ordered with rows of terraced houses and three-storey flatted blocks grouped in regimented fashion around large grassy squares.

Like many later Spence buildings, the Natural Philosophy building (now known as the Physics block) combines a strict geometric rigour with elements of the organic tradition.

For the external finish Spence advised against brick because it weathers badly in Scotland, it was associated with a lower class of building (such as cinemas and garages) and it was expensive in Scotland because of the high cost of carriage. Stone was the only alternative, and he recom-mended Portland stone on the grounds of cost and quality.[10]

With Spence's disciplined architecture of superblocks, overtures towards straight-edged, smooth-planed buildings and application of the Radburn system of traffic segregation for the first time in Scotland, the estate at Bannerfield is an important landmark in the development of post-war council housing.

Four such squares are linked by a tree-lined central boulevard with smaller squares to the north.

Compared to Spence's housing at Shepperton and Sunbury-on-Thames, designed at about the same time, his development at Selkirk with its strictly orthogonal layout and repetitive units recalls European rather than British precedents. Though Spence struggled to enliven the buildings with delicate porches, windows picked out in concrete frames and exaggerated chimney stacks, the overall effect is one of geometric order and uniformity.

Above right Housing, Bannerfield estate, Selkirk, 1949.
Right Aerial perspective by Spence of his masterplan of 1946 for the Bannerfield estate, Selkirk. Notice the emphasis upon disciplined layout even at relatively low residential density.

Housing at Sunbury-on-Thames, Middlesex, 1950. Notice the lively composition when viewed on the diagonal. Work of this quality and at Selkirk won Spence a special prize for housing design at the Festival of Britain.

Spence's schools stand in marked contrast to the Hertfordshire schools developed at the same time and designed to be constructed employing the CLASP system, e.g. Templewood School, Welwyn, 1949. Where Spence exploits – with an artist's sensibility – light, space, interior volume and sensuous quality of materials, the CLASP schools were conceived with the minimum of circulation space and the maximum of flexibility. Also, while Duncanrig School gives the impression of a unified whole, the CLASP schools, driven by system rather than artistic verve, sometimes recall a collection of separate, mechanistic and often disjointed buildings.

to create a landmark for the new town by placing the accommodation in a tower, an idea later abandoned on advice from the Scottish Office.[2] After several designs had been proposed, construction began in 1953. The circulation of the school was organised around a long, wide corridor acting like a central spine linking a series of classrooms placed to the north and south. Between the classrooms lengths of corridor opened the school to views over – what was then – open countryside. The rhythm of containment and release established by this alternating pattern is typical of the architect, though its effect was reduced by the authorities who insisted on introducing fire partitions into the main school corridor. In plan the solid and void relationship is developed further by Spence's choice of building materials. Rusticated lengths of rubble wall and areas of harl contrast with large sheets of glass set in thin frames which create the effect of transparent screens. Where staircases occur these are lightweight, projecting outwards either as metal spiral stairs or as thin cantilevered structures.

At right angles to the main corridor Spence placed a wedge-shaped assembly hall and pair of gymnasiums. The angle of the wedge projects outwards to form the configuration of the forecourt at the main school entrance in a fashion reminiscent of the interior-exterior plan arrangement at Gribloch. Immediately inside the entrance a large mural by William Crosbie, depicting life and industry, stands on the outer face of the assembly hall to confront visitors.

Duncanrig School shows growing maturity. The play of architectural mass set tantalisingly against transparency; the double and single heights inside; the rough masonry construction alongside smooth finishes all suggest that Spence was an artist in building rather than an architect in the traditional sense.

A university and hospital architect

In common with most universities in the 1950s Edinburgh University sought to accommodate government policy to increase student numbers and redirect teaching towards engineering and the sciences. Early in 1954 the University decided to abandon its earlier policy of suburban expansion, especially southwards along Dalkeith Road where science teaching had become established in the pre-war years. The Principal, Sir Edward Appleton, harboured an ambition (whose origin lay in a city development plan adopted in 1948) to provide a central heart for the University around George Square where a new library, lecture rooms, examination hall, chapel, union buildings and staff club were to be grouped.[3] To realise his

Perspective drawing by Spence, prepared in 1955, of the sequence of courtyards extending from George Square eastwards. The modern character of the University of Edinburgh was effectively established by Spence in a sequence of perspective paintings which supported his masterplan report. Note also Spence's Humanist tendencies in allowing the trees of George Square to continue to dominate the view and in providing sculpture and water to enliven the spaces created.

Edinburgh University

Proposed plan (bottom) *and perspective* (below) *of chapel for Edinburgh University, 1956. The tower is shown facing the junction of Bristo Street and Marshall Street. The entrance from the west is via a porte-cochère.*

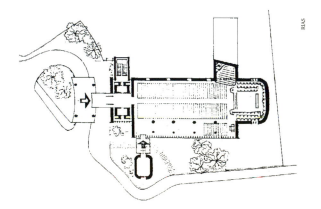

Spence gave appropriate form to Appleton's vision for George Square with modern buildings on all but the west side. Pride of place was reserved for the design of a new library to be built on the south side. Spence's library design, at the time a far cry from the final building itself, consisted of a five-storey block divided into alternate bays of glazing and solid panels of sandstone with a dramatic flat-domed reading room penetrating through the roof. In a perspective, taken from a viewpoint in the Meadows, the dome rises above the treetops to act as a landmark from afar. The penetration of architectural volumes and the recessing of an entrance cube is typical of the solid and void relationship which characterises his work.

The masterplan by Spence reversed many of the propositions which underpinned the Holden Plan. Besides moving the choice of site for a new library, Spence proposed a grouping of union buildings and chapel south of Lothian Street. His interest in processional routes finds expression in the sequence of courtyards, teaching blocks and towers linking George Square eastward to Buccleuch Street. His ability to translate Appleton's grandiose vision into a development for which the University won planning permission, in spite of growing opposition within the city, says a great deal about Spence's persuasive powers as orator and graphic artist. The hardwood model prepared and his four large perspectives provided the development framework for the next twenty years.

The new library was a major departure from the original intention. Developed in collaboration with Spence's partner in the Edinburgh office, Hardie Glover, and his assistant (later partner) Andrew Merrylees, the library now consists of horizontal layers of concrete balconies cantilevered over cliffs of glazing in place of the earlier and more romantic proposal which was possibly influenced by Asplund. The red sandstone of the 1955 perspectives had been replaced, in 1967, by white

concrete, and the shallow dome by a flat roof punctuated only by plant rooms. The decade between the adoption of the Spence perspectives and the maturing of ideas for the library saw the building undergo changes in form and authorship. Though Spence maintained overall control, details were developed by Glover and Merrylees in the Edinburgh office. The method of working was typical of Spence. He would produce *'rough but vivid sketches indicating the general form of the building'*[9] which were then worked up by partners and assistants. One detail was lost in the transition: Spence's original idea of employing double-height glazed panels to offset the stratified horizontality of the floors was abandoned.

The new library is remarkable for its graceful, almost Japanese, elegance of line which belies the actual size and bulk of a building eight storeys high at the Meadows' façade. The building has public fronts on all sides and, by extending the 'brise soleil' of projecting concrete balconies on the southern elevation to those on the north (where solar projection is not justified in the Scottish climate), the balance of horizontal and vertical forces is maintained (see p.55). The result, functionally questionable, is an architectural success. The uncompromising, if mannered, application of bold forms drawn from the Modern Movement vindicates Spence's earlier conviction that contemporary design would not look ill at ease in the square. A sense of space, light and matter pervades the interior, particularly in the double-height entrance hall and there are splendid views out over George Square to the north and the Meadows to the south. With central circulation stairs

Edinburgh University: perspective drawing by Spence of view of proposed expansion from The Meadows (1955).

The 1950s and 1960s was a period which saw student numbers in Britain grow rapidly from around 80,000 in 1950 to 300,000 in 1970. Under the influence of the Robbins Committee, the British Government agreed to expand existing universities, to create nine new ones from the bones of colleges of advanced technology and to build a further six universities on greenfield sites. Spence benefited more than most architects from this expansion: he was employed to conceive one of the largest new universities (Sussex) and to design several major buildings in others.

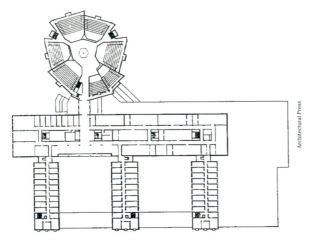

Institute of Physics and Mathematics, Edinburgh University, 1960. The lecture theatres (top) are reminiscent of works by Alvar Aalto in their free form and contrast with the rationally planned staff and seminar rooms.

Falmer House, University of Sussex, 1958, designed with expressive colours and forms of concrete segmental arches and soft red brick.

and lifts encased in heavy concrete, the solid/void relationship, dear to the architect, finds expression on the inside. The final building, nevertheless, confirms Spence's talent for producing monuments of power and simplicity in quiet and leafy settings.

Spence had introduced the spirit and abstract forms of contemporary architecture to George Square. He delivered what Principal Appleton had sought – a modern campus with a centre for social life where *'interior lines of communication'* could exert their influence. He achieved this without the restrictions of a formally adopted development plan. His approach was to form secondary squares rather than streets around which accommodation could be grouped in order to create what he later called the *'sense of a university'*.[10] Spence had already displayed his facility for 'place' making (see p.39) and at Edinburgh employed a sequence of linked courtyards which stitched new, largely monumental, teaching accommodation into the older fabric of the city. Some proposals were not realised, such as the dramatic design for a university chapel in Bristo Street (see pp.66 & 76), and other buildings were designed in detail by quite different architects.

At Edinburgh University, Spence was given the opportunity to display his full range of talents as town planner, conceptual designer, architect of individual buildings and interior designer (as in the conversion of buildings in Chambers Street to serve as the Staff Club). His abilities as a university architect of vision were quickly sought elsewhere notably at Sussex, Southampton, Durham and Newcastle where the powerful, rhythmic forms of Spence's architecture remain also as a legacy of educational expansion in the post-war period. Buildings for Sussex University display his talents to the full. Here, concrete barrel-vaults and sensuous brickwork demonstrate the influence of Le Corbusier's 'Maisons Jaoul', and their forms are applied at an exaggerated scale to produce

RIAS

St Aidan's College, Durham, designed by the Edinburgh office in 1962. The combination of transparency and structural muscularity recalls the porch at Coventry Cathedral and Sussex University.

collegiate architecture of monumental intent. The choice of materials, the colour of the finishes and the relationship between buildings and landscape evoke the sense of a new university which is both traditional and progressive. This was an aptitude used by Spence at Southampton where his campus masterplan and individual buildings such as the arts building and animal house have a real sense of composition and feel for materials. Where Sussex is fashioned largely of brick, Southampton is concrete and stone, yet on both campuses the powerful volumes and sensuous rhythms of his architecture testify to the architect's growing maturity.

Spence's flair for modern functional design tempered by regional building sensibilities is evident also at Edinburgh's Western General Hospital where his practice was appointed to design new operating theatres (in 1956) and further hospital

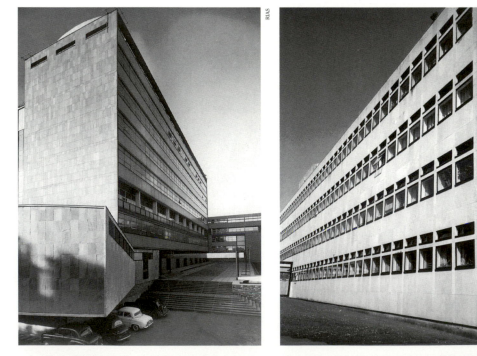

RIAS

University of Southampton

Physics building, University of Newcastle, designed by the Edinburgh office of Basil Spence, Glover and Ferguson in 1960.

Simple lines of Southampton University, 1960, designed by the London office of Basil Spence, Bonnington and Collins.

accommodation (1957-67). Here the exploitation of daringly expressed structures (as in the building of the new operating theatres on massive legs to lift them over the old theatres) and the clever play of textures (stone, brick, concrete, harl) illustrate Spence's continuing search for spirited yet honest architecture.

Growing assurance at Newhaven

In 1955 Spence was appointed to redevelop an area of insanitary fishermen's houses near the waterfront at Newhaven. Commissioned by Edinburgh Corporation, his task was to prepare housing plans for about 160 flats at medium density as part of a larger comprehensive redevelopment area scheme by Ian G Lindsay & Partners. To the west fragments of old Newhaven survived where roughly finished sandstone houses with front steps were grouped around small courtyards with wynds placed at right angles to the sea. Spence, in characteristic fashion, responded to this context with a lively collection of two-, three- and four-storey flats, all with carefully articulated stairs, retaining walls and ramps of local stone, arranged around a square sloping down to the Firth of Forth. The formality of the scheme is softened by greenery and the stepping of individual blocks down a steep slope. The use of a large central courtyard hidden from the main road is reminiscent of both the later stages of Dunbar and Bannerfield and allows Spence to set picturesque details within an urban plan. The delicate angles of balconies with their thin (Festival of Britain) railings, window frames and exposed floor slabs, all used in conjunction with rough harled walls and large panels of granite setts, give the development both a ruggedness and a picturesque quality in keeping with the locality.

Spence also employs colour and texture in a fresh and invigorating fashion. By drawing on the tradition of painted

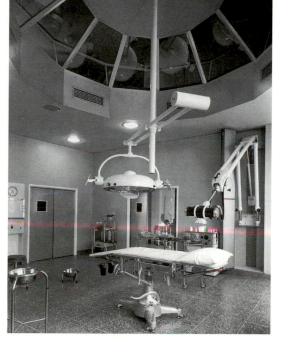

Interior of new operating theatre at Western General Hospital, Edinburgh, 1956-8.

When completed in 1957 the development won a Saltire Award for housing. This, combined with the earlier housing prize given to him at the Festival of Britain, established Spence as one of the major designers of urban housing of his generation.

Newhaven flats for Edinburgh, 1955.

At Coventry Spence recommended the appointment of Ove Arup, whom he told the reconstruction committee was the *'best engineer to understand the aesthetic point of view, and a brilliant professional'*. Spence recounts the *Phoenix at Coventry* that Arup understood immediately the *'subtler meanings of the design'* and helped the architect see the vault as separate from the cathedral roof. This separation allowed the nave columns to be designed simply to hold the vault with the perimeter walls supporting the roof. Arup was also responsible for the idea of the pin joint between column and floor, initially as a glass sphere, but later in bronze.

fishermen's housing in the East of Scotland, the architect exploits the effect of dense colour viewed against natural materials such as stone and slate. Within the courtyard, areas of red, brown, yellow and blue harl resonate against the grey northern light.

A cathedral and church architect

Unexpected success in winning the Coventry Cathedral competition in 1951, and Spence's spirited defence of what many saw as a design that was too modern, had the effect of projecting him into the public consciousness. This led to many commissions for new churches, some of which were in Scotland. The Coventry design, developed single-handedly through the night accompanied by the Brandenburg Concertos, was to prove a turning point in his life. If a handful of bishops and senior members of the architectural establishment had doubts over the frankly expressed forms and contemporary spirit of the new cathedral, nevertheless, younger clergy praised the design. On radio and television, Spence conveyed the impression of a cultured and urbane architect anxious to build a Cathedral of *'one's own time, to serve the people living now'*. If his enthusiasm for modern materials and methods of construction, coupled with his understanding of the spirituality of church architecture, proved popular, he had one further attraction: he recognised that church architecture was a collaborative endeavour involving clergy, artists and craftsmen. Spence regarded them all as essential to the creation of a great religious building.

Spence intended his cathedral to represent the New Testament with the gaunt ruins symbolising the Old. He conceived the design as telling the story of the Bible – the interior being open, well lit, simple in character and enriched with modern Christian icons. The 'idea seed' as he called it grew in the first five minutes of his visit to Coventry and he

Perspective drawing of 1952 showing the relationship between the old and new cathedrals at Coventry. The majestic entrance porch appealed to the assessors.

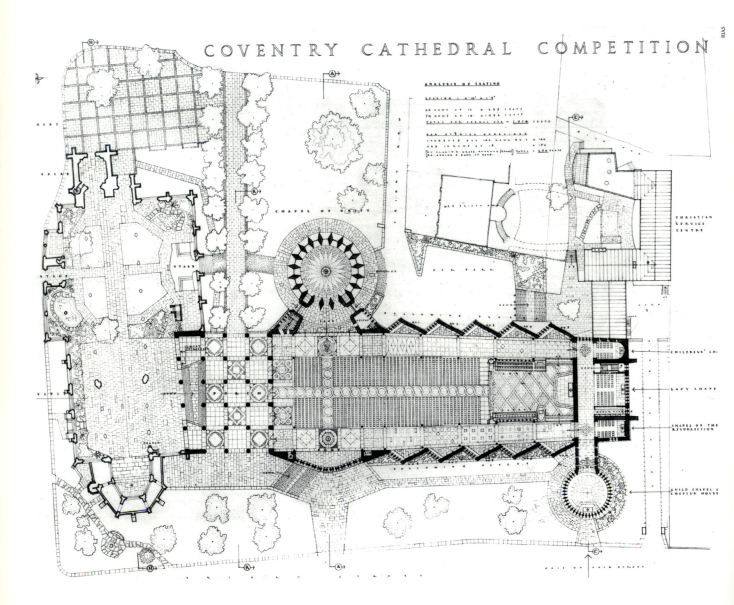

COVENTRY CATHEDRAL COMPETITION

was so convinced of its validity that he *'never considered an alternative'*.[11] Edward Maufe, the chief assessor and architect of Guildford Cathedral, said of Spence's design that by keeping the ruins of the old cathedral and dividing them from the new by a huge glazed porch, by using the existing tower to counterbalance the new nave, by the careful proportioning of the elements, the architect had achieved a design of *'outstanding excellence'*. The play of solid architectural mass, transparent walls of glass set within chunky stone frames, the orchestration of light, procession and contextual references (the spacing of the porch columns and window mullions reflect those in the bombed cathedral) was extremely skilled. It was a skill he employed a decade later at the Rome Embassy designed in 1960 and constructed in 1970-1. Here the adjacent Porta Pia by Michelangelo provided the basis for the proportions and structural rhythm of the new chancery.[12] As at Coventry, the professional press criticised the design but, on completion, the building quickly attracted admirers for its subtlety of composition within a sensitive historic setting.

The underlying simplicity was achieved by deploying a reinforced concrete vault to span a wide aisleless nave capable of seating 1374. Tall, elegant tapered columns of steel cased in sculpted concrete support metaphorically a faceted vault with ribs of precast, post-stressed concrete. Angled walls of pink-grey stone contrast with the smooth plaster ceiling and direct light via colourful windows to the altar. The compositional unity and expressive use of materials reflected something of the spirit of Gothic architecture without abandoning modern principles. In his attempted reconciliation of the two generations of cathedral architecture, many critics accused Spence of being too referential. However, Lewis Mumford (who accompanied Spence round the building) observed that the building *'vibrates longer and with deeper resonance than many other works of modern architecture'*.[13]

Although Coventry was widely praised on completion, the initial design was often attacked in lay and professional circles. Spence's wife Joan protected him from much adverse mail which came to the office, sorting through the letters and allowing Basil to see only those which were favourably disposed to the design. Joan Spence, being the tougher character, was the power behind the throne and shielded Basil from criticism. According to his partner, Hardie Glover, she increasingly became the dominant personality, willing Basil to stand by his principles at Coventry and elsewhere whenever his designs hit opposition.

RIAS

Between 1950 and 1965 Spence designed three churches and a crematorium in Scotland, and nearly a dozen others in England. In each Scottish work he exploits the design elements of angled walls, usually evening sunlight, thick masonry construction and internal space which sets dark mysterious volumes against areas bathed in light. Two churches, that at St Andrew's, Clermiston (1957), near Edinburgh, and the earlier unbuilt church of St Ninian and St Martin (1951), at Whithorn, adopt the simple linear nave of Coventry Cathedral, with its focus on an altar which stands in front of a tapestry hanging from heavy stonework. The Whithorn church appears a precursor to Coventry (it was designed months before Spence had won the competition) in that the angled walls were designed to shed light on the altar. Influenced by the tradition of St Ninian's first church at Whithorn being a cave, Spence responded by creating an asymmetrical cavernous nave and gave it a surface of rounded paving stones, which appeared washed smooth as if by the sea.

More organic in spirit is another unrealised church: a chapel and congregational hall for Edinburgh University designed in 1955. Intended as a landmark for the area north of George

RIAS

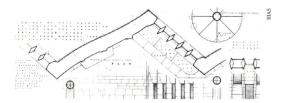

RIAS

Top *Perspective drawing of Coventry Cathedral painted by Spence soon after winning the competition.*
Above *Sketch submitted as part of the competition drawings showing how wall, sunlight and religious iconography were related in modern fashion.*
Top right *Coventry Cathedral rising from the ashes of wartime bombing in 1953. Success at Coventry led to Spence moving house from Edinburgh to London.*

Square, the design had the simplicity, directness and spatial mood of a Celtic chapel. The large hall with seating for 1,000 was to be engulfed within rubble-clad stone walls which were angled inwards, reminiscent of a Scottish castle. A free-standing campanile of massive masonry construction was to be linked, Coventry fashion, to the nave by a simple glazed entrance porch.

St Andrew's, Clermiston, has less mystery but more panache. Here Spence conceived a simple rectangular church to seat 400 with an adjacent smaller hall and free-standing bell-tower separated by glazed screens. The whole composition of balanced stone and rendered parts sits on a sandstone base bisected by a sweeping flight of steps. The arrangement of unfolding volumes and cross-processional routes seems deliberately to gain visual impact from the low angled sun of the north. Diagonal shafts of sunlight point a visitor through from the western approach via a sequence of connected spaces to a simple but elegant nave. The altar is the obvious point of focus, flanked by an archway of angled stone walls now covered with creepers.

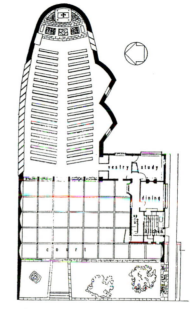

Architect & Building News

plan at ground floor

RIAS

Above *Unrealised design for church of St Ninian and St Martin, Whithorn, 1951. The influence of Coventry can be seen in the angled walls and entrance court. This design and Coventry proceeded in parallel.*
Left *St Andrew's, Clermiston, Edinburgh (1957), a composition of finely judged contrasts.*

RIAS

Above and right *Mortonhall Crematorium designed by Spence in 1962. (Notice how the plan is arranged to exploit the qualities of sunlight.)*

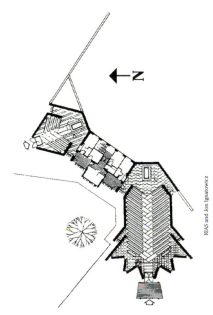

RIAS and Jon Ignatowicz

Writing about Spence's churches in 1958, Edward Mills rightly compared their underlying spirit with the work of Le Corbusier.[14] Mortonhall Crematorium, designed in 1962 with the assistance of Hardie Glover, is the climax of this series of bold, yet expressive and atmospheric churches. The site for the crematorium was in woodland at the southern edge of Edinburgh. The long approach through dense tree planting evokes memories of Gunnar Asplund's Stockholm Crematorium of 1939, which Spence appears to acknowledge in his site planning. The crematorium, chapel and waiting shelter are arranged as a loose triangle of free-standing structures united in their forms and materials (siliceous concrete) to each other. In the theatrical handling of interior wall-planes and the use of shafted and diffused light, the angular crematorium chapel suggests a debt to Ronchamp. As with the Whithorn church and Coventry Cathedral, light is deflected to direct attention to the altar. Spence orientated the windows to focus afternoon sunlight on the catafalque using stained glass to induce sparkling colour. Spence struck a balance between functional efficacy and the needs of the spirit, using his compositional prowess and love of architectural orchestration.

RIAS

In the design of churches Spence uses light as a tactile material in its own right, employing sunlight to punctuate the neutrality of the nave.

Interior of chapel of Mortonhall Crematorium, Edinburgh.

Chapter 4 · The 1960s and after – An Architect of Authority

RIAS

Gorbals blocks (known subsequently as Queen Elizabeth Square) showing the powerful rhythms established by Spence's approach to high-rise living.

Enjoying growing wealth and professional popularity, President of the Royal Institute of British Architects in 1958-60, Spence's flamboyant style, self-confidence and persuasiveness had won friends in government, with influential clients, with the clergy and the public. For the first time since the war, Basil Spence was one modern architect the general public could readily name when asked.

During the 1960s Spence's architecture grew in power and authority, as a comparison between his proposals for the library at Edinburgh University of 1955 with the realised design of 1967 suggests. The visual strength and compositional drama which found expression in two notable projects, the Gorbals flats and Glasgow Airport, is evident also in later works. That Spence displayed greater confidence following Coventry Cathedral is hardly surprising: what makes his work unusual, however, is the combination of compositional swagger with recurrent organic design tendencies. The Gorbals blocks reinterpret the Glasgow tenement in heroic massed form and his Canongate flats combine a weighty architectural language of square-cut balconies and pierced windows with elements of traditional Scottish building such as rendered stonework, pitched roofs and pend entrances.

His manner and lifestyle changed with the growing authority in his architecture. The cigars became larger and more frequently smoked, the fondness for fine wine and good food increased as did his liking for chauffeur-driven cars. By the 1960s his two children had left the family home. His daughter Gillian married his junior partner in the London office, Anthony Blee. His appointment of Professor of Architecture at the Royal Academy between 1961 and 1968 was largely a ceremonial affair which Spence enjoyed as much for its social contact as academic content. Knighted in 1960, largely on the basis of Coventry, he became, in 1962, Britain's only architect

OM and the first after Lutyens who received the same honour in 1942.

Although Spence and his wife Joan continued to live occasionally above the office in Canonbury, the focus of domestic life moved to Beaulieu in Hampshire where he designed the family home in 1961. With its easy access to Solent Water, the Hampshire house satisfied Spence's growing appetite for sailing. In 1964 he built a villa for himself at Banalbufar in Majorca and used this for what holidays he could, given the demands of a growing number of clients. In what must have been a hectic period for him, Spence continued to find time for sailing, sketching, collecting works of art and preparing lightning, atmospheric perspectives of his different designs, many of which were displayed at the Royal Academy summer shows.

Spence received his OM a year before the sculptor Henry Moore and two years after Graham Sutherland, artist of the Coventry tapestry. The OM, limited to twenty-four living members, is conferred *'for exceptionally meritorious services in Our Army or Navy or towards the advancement of the Arts, Literature or Science'.*

Portrait of Sir Basil Spence in 1960, the year of his knighthood, as President of RIBA.

The family home at Beaulieu, designed by Spence in 1961.

Spence's demands extended also to dress: staff hurriedly changed into mustard-coloured ties, charcoal-grey suits and Hush Puppies as their director arrived. Although Spence was a flamboyant dresser with a penchant for bow ties, he liked his staff to wear a more sober unofficial uniform.

Spence did not abandon Scotland or Scottish work. While earlier on Scotland had provided the mainstay of his practice, by the 1960s the proportion of work north of the border was only about a quarter of his practice's total output. Spence's visits to the Moray Place office were, however, at least monthly and he kept a close eye on design output. On more than one occasion he was unhappy when he discovered his sketch elevations had been modified. Staff in Edinburgh were not always aware in advance of his visits and kept a watchful eye out for the Jenner's catering van which delivered the buffet lunch to bolster a busy morning travelling by train from London. He could be sharp and demanding with his staff, mixing natural affability with determination to ensure his particular architectural vision was stamped upon every project. Not all staff bowed to his aesthetic demands: Andrew Merrylees won his horizontal balconies at Edinburgh University Library against Spence's wish for vertical mullions and found himself soon after promoted to a partner, but others with design ambition left the practice.

Spence at the Gorbals

In his Gorbals appointment of 1958 Spence sought to *'civilise the tenement'* and bring it up-to-date in modern high-rise form.[1] The Gorbals, established as a fashionable new town similar to Edinburgh in 1780, had deteriorated into slums before the war. What remained at the time of Spence's appointment was insanitary flats subdivided from the remains of large, gracious tenements which lined once handsome streets. After an initial interview with Glasgow Corporation, Spence travelled to Marseilles to visit Le Corbusier's 'Unité d'Habitation'.[2] His subsequent design for the two linked Gorbals blocks shows the influence of Unité with their maisonettes, double-height gallery gardens and exaggerated concrete pylons which sweep up from the ground in almost Gothic fashion. The use of

RIAS

Queen Elizabeth II unveiling a plaque on completion of the Gorbals blocks in 1962. Spence was not present at the ceremony.

RIAS

groups of four linked gardens in the sky where Spence thought residents would grow plants, hang out washing, gossip and give the baby an airing,[3] was further evidence of the architect's romantic leanings. Four hundred families were originally housed in the development comprising a population of about 2,000, not dissimilar to a small Scottish town. Spence sought to provide community facilities, not on the roof as the exemplar of Unité would suggest, but in a nearby courtyard.

He compared his blocks to *'ocean liners'*, telling a meeting of the Glasgow Housing Committee that, on wash days, the building would look *'like a great ship in full sail'*.[4] The nautical analogy, evident in massing and certain details, draws upon Le

Gorbals blocks (left) a few years prior to their demolition in 1993. The iconography of ocean liners is evident in this view.

A L Hunter Photography

Above *Interior of an apartment. Double heights and simple thoughtful design (including sliding doors to the kitchen) characterised the Gorbals blocks.* Right *Cartoon by Louis Hellman from Building Design published four months before the demolition of Spence's Gorbals blocks.*

Corbusier's fascination with the Cunard liner 'Aquitania' which housed 3,600 people in a self-contained, well-lit structure with promenades and clean healthy lines. The pair of almost linked slab blocks built by Spence in 1962 were infinitely more accomplished as formal architecture than the remaining 140 high-rise council blocks in the city, most of which were results of contractor package deals. The maisonettes were arranged scissor fashion about a central corridor designed to act as 'streets-in-the-air' on alternate floors. This section allowed Spence to reduce corridor space and increase the area of the balconies which, in true Le Corbusier fashion, were of double height, finished in shuttered concrete.

The Spence towers expressed their structure in a bold fashion as gargantuan concrete pylons physically and visually transmitting loads to the ground, ending in wonderful splayed pilotis like the legs of a giant rhinoceros. The well-articulated structure designed by the Danish engineer, Povl Ahm, in Ove Arup's office, and the distinction made between feet, midriff and top, gives clear expression to the *'tall block artistically considered'*. This expressive play of columns, panels and apertures made a lively composition

Louis Hellman

especially when the sun shone. The gables and skyline were likewise animated, creating a powerful silhouette when viewed from across the Clyde.

Subsequently known as Queen Elizabeth Square (in recognition of the laying of the foundation stone by the Queen in 1962), the Spence design proved prone to vandalism. In spite of their heroic monumentality and reinterpretation of the tenement into modern high-rise blocks, the Gorbals towers were demolished in 1993.

Canongate, Edinburgh

Spence also conceived housing on a smaller scale in Edinburgh's Canongate flats (1966) which arouse interest in the context of the organic tradition of modern Scottish architecture. Panels of rubble stonework alternate with areas of brightly coloured harl punctured periodically by deep square-cut windows and wavy balconies. A powerful and severe rhythm is established, relieved

Above *Interior of the street through the centre of the block.* Left *Redevelopment of the Canongate, Edinburgh, to designs by Spence, 1966. Rugged natural materials used in modern fashion characterise the scheme.*

Scottish Widows is a building of cerebral rather than sensory interest. It is easily overlooked today but, when conceived in 1960, was one of the most ambitious urban buildings in Scotland. The design maintains the Modernist doctrine, which Spence sought to follow, of externally expressing the interior functions.

Designed in collaboration with Andrew Renton in 1957 and constructed in 1959, Thorn House derives its podium and tower form from Lever House in New York by Gordon Burnshaft. It was the first building in London to employ this spatially fluid arrangement which, besides maintaining street enclosure for the pedestrian, releases the tower from the orthodox straight-jacket of the city. In the design of the tower Spence and Renton balance the horizontal lines of glazing bars against the vertical lines of structural columns which are taken through to the roof twelve storeys higher as an open skeleton of concrete frames. The tower, clad in grey marble, contrasts pleasantly with the black marble of the two-storey podium which contained Thorn's shop.

at the ground by segmental arched concrete canopies, echoing former Renaissance arches. Despite its historic references, the development is almost Scandinavian in abstraction. The rear elevation, with its rough concrete cubic balconies and deep overhangs, borrows design elements from the Gorbals blocks. Even with shallow pitched roofs the skyline is lively, and at times elaborate, with hints of castellation where the sandstone walls project beyond the eaves. Compared to the more sedate blocks built at about the same time further up the Canongate by Robert Hurd, this development displays the assurance of an architect alive to the spirit of Scottish Renaissance architecture but reluctant to simply copy. In its completed form, some of the vigour and crisp geometric forms of the first proposals in 1955 were lost.[5]

Scottish Widows, St Andrew Square, Edinburgh

While Spence was designing the Canongate flats, he was also appointed to design the Scottish Widows' building in St Andrew Square, Edinburgh. It was a major commission and the first substantial office project in Scotland. The design, realised in 1962, is a disciplined, if rather restrained, addition to the square, with a sober elevation that turns along Rose Street opposite Jenner's department store. Unlike other projects by Spence, there are few correspondences to either the organic tradition or that of the modern Scots Revival. Here a grid of windows framed in grey marble sits on a shiny black base of polished granite. There is a large entrance cube punched, a little off-centre, into the front elevation matching a similar Classical treatment opposite. The entrance is reached by a straight flight of steps which leads from the pavement to a double-height inner foyer – also in black and dramatically punctuated by a round lift-shaft encircled by a curved stair. As at Causewayside garage the circle within a cube reappears as a favoured Spence motif. Here, not only are primary geometric shapes played off against each other, but black is set in contrast against grey and white in a fashion recalling Thorn House in London (1960) designed by Spence and Renton.

Scottish Widows' building, St Andrew Square, Edinburgh. The use of a cylinder with an encircling staircase appeared in his design for the Cleghorn store in George Street nearly 30 years earlier.

*Glasgow Airport, 1962-6. Powerful
structure was increasingly used by
Spence for its formal rather than
its functional quality.*

Glasgow Airport

In 1962 Spence was appointed by the Ministry of Aviation to
design Abbotsinch Airport (later named Glasgow Airport),
seven miles west of Glasgow. The appointment was personal to
Sir Basil himself. He undertook the commission from the
Edinburgh, rather than the London, office. After an initial
briefing, then early sketches prepared in London, Spence with
Hardie Glover as his senior partner evolved the design with
little additional support.[6]

The site plan at Glasgow was strongly influenced by the layout
of Gatwick, designed just two years earlier.[7] Both airports
adopted the pattern of a central terminus with right-angled and

cranked piers leading to the departure gates. At the terminus, Spence turned a utilitarian programme into a cathedral-like structure with widely spaced columns, almost ceremonial staircases and a boldly expressed overhanging concrete roof. He took advantage of the long unbroken south-facing façade, which would face the planned M8 motorway, by exploiting the structural rhythms and shadows cast by the arched roof.

Spence used scale and rhythm to give his terminal the presence required: sixteen bays, expressed in lively spirit by a cantilevered concrete roof. The regular grid of tall, slender columns and the bold segmental arches give unity and coherence to a host of different interior functions.

Spence brought a sense of theatre to Glasgow Airport to help with the functional task of moving people through a terminal. Although the details of the design are not always his, there is an architectural consistency which unites the project. The board-shuttered concrete is truly of the early Sixties, the heroic, mannered arches hint at the Brutalism of London's South Bank (then under construction) and the grand flight of stairs leading from concourse to mezzanine floor areas has a scale in keeping with the aviation age.

As with Coventry and Sussex, structure, light and space are the elements which provide the fundamental order and framework to Spence's monumental architecture. At Sussex, designed in the same year, a similar pattern of large concrete arches articulates the elevation of the library block in particular and exploits the rhythms of sunlight and shadow.

University of Sussex

University of Sussex, 1960. Under the influence of Le Corbusier's Maisons Jaoul, the segmented arch and muscular construction were recurring themes in Spence's architecture.

NMRS

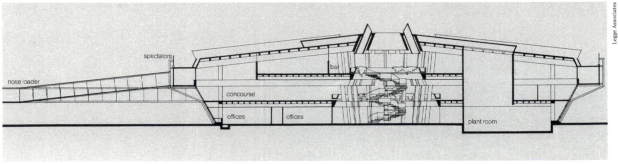

Legge Associates

Top and above *Model and section of proposed design for the Satellite Pier at Glasgow Airport, 1970.*

In 1970 the office designed the Satellite Pier, fashioned with the same clarity and sense of architectural drama. Here a circular, top-lit pavilion with angled walls of tinted glass allowed planes to taxi in from any angle.

St James' Square, Edinburgh

In 1964 Spence became involved in the controversial plans to redevelop St James' Square at the eastern edge of Edinburgh's New Town. The intention was to form a major office and retail quarter near the top of Leith Walk. After a design brief had been drawn up by Edinburgh Corporation, three developers were invited to submit proposals each using a different architect – Sir Basil Spence, Glover and Ferguson; Ian Burke Associates, and Hugh Martin and Partners. The developer Hammerson employed Spence's office which drew up a scheme preferred by the Royal Fine Art Commission for Scotland. The Commission had earlier argued that architectural merit, rather than tenders for the land, should be the basis for the award of the contract. But the Spence scheme was not adopted, in spite of the Commission's support for the design, since, according to the town council, it entailed *'a minor deviation'* from Edinburgh Corporation's preferred road layout.[8] In the event, the council's highway engineers thwarted what was widely considered the best urban design solution. Spence, like many architects before and since, had departed from a detail of a road configuration on the grounds of civic design and found the success of his plans in the competition jeopardised. As the Royal Fine Art Commission for Scotland subsequently noted, the winning design did not attain the architectural and civic standard imperatively required of the site and architectural merit could not be said to have won the day.

Chapter 5 · An appraisal of Spence

The writer of *The Times* obituary for Sir Basil Spence summed up his contribution to the architecture of his generation through his buildings, his sense of style and his manner of working by noting that he was rather more an architect of the eighteenth than the twentieth century.[1] One suspects Spence would have been pleased with such a judgement. He appreciated the masculine, strong and pictorial elements of architecture and believed that architects should be *'inventive and forward looking'*. His vision, creativity and desire to control the full design of a project – from how a building sits in the landscape to details such as the design of light fittings – place him in the mould, if not the century, of Robert Adam.

His marked personal philosophy of design was outlined in a

Glasgow Royal Infirmary, 1972-80, in the Spence tradition of powerfully expressed structural rhythms. Built posthumously.

RIAS

number of lectures. He was preoccupied as much with interiors as exteriors; with proportion, rhythm and chiaroscuro – how light filters through windows to bathe interiors in light.[2] He was keen to exploit the natural textures of materials arguing, for instance, that the 'stoniness' of stone should be expressed. In some ways, he may be classified with the organic tradition of late nineteenth- and twentieth-century architecture – working with local materials and wishing to sustain regional traditions of building. Many of his earlier buildings derive their strength and character from an appreciation of Scotland's architectural heritage. This finds expression not only in the choice of materials and sensitivity to location, but in the powerful contrast of solid building mass against space and volume. The latter tendency, derived from elements of the Scots Revival of the pre-war years, allowed Spence to mature as a creator of building forms rather than merely as a designer. His admiration of Scottish Medieval buildings which he praised for their *'almost purely sculptural basis to the forms developed'*[3] is the key to understanding Spence's approach to design.

High as Spence's reputation was a decade before his death, he was rather more popular with the general public than in architectural circles. There were professional critics who did not like his design style. The gifts of draughtsmanship and oratory which he used to persuade committees and individual clients to adopt certain plans were regarded by some design purists as unworthy of a great architect. His subtle sense of space and of the relationship of buildings to the landscape were lasting strengths, yet for some critics the subtlety was expressed more readily in atmospheric perspective sketches than in atmospheric buildings. He placed emphasis upon the *'initial pictorial conception'*[4] believing that the architect's prime duty was to address visual matters. In an age where architectural character was expected to emerge in response to

RIAS

Proctor & Gamble building, Newcastle, designed by the Edinburgh office in 1962. Water is used to provide an ambiguity of surfaces at the building edge and the circular fountain discs offset the linearity of the façade. The debt to Arne Jacobsen's St Catherine's College, Oxford, is evident.

Above *Detail of a staircase of Edinburgh University Staff Club, 1967.*
Top right *Perspective view through porch of Coventry Cathedral painted by Spence soon after winning the competition.*
Right *Albyn Restaurant, Edinburgh, 1968. Where Spence could not exploit powerful contrasts in space and volume, he was happy to apply paint in contrasting vivid patterns.*

a functional programme, Spence's buildings were considered to lack intellectual rigour. Meanwhile, as a consequence of his conviction that bold modern buildings were compatible with the perimeter of the London parks, Spence became increasingly isolated in his views and, in his last years, both the profession and public seemed to turn against, arguably, the leading architect of the post-war period.

Spence's primary regard for appearance is more in keeping with the spirit of our post-industrial (or should I say post-Modern) age. His propensity for dramatic outline and contrasting volumes and textures, suggests an artist using building as a medium. Coventry Cathedral, the Gorbals flats, Mortonhall Crematorium, Sussex University and the Rome Embassy are the buildings of an architect with the sensibility of a sculptor. The feeling of strength, the handling of light, the interior spatial volumes, exterior shapes and the contextual references made in them were exceptional in their expressive qualities in post-war Britain. Spence was as conscious of his Scottish roots as he was of North European Expressionism and Le Corbusier's progressive, metropolitan, mechanistic monumentality. He bridged the two worlds of Alvar Aalto and Le Corbusier, blending a Nordic regard for materials, site and nature with the heroic forms and plastic expression of Unité and Ronchamp.

Spence was not a political idealogue and did not align himself with circles such as Congrès Internationaux d'Architecture Moderne (CIAM) or its English offshoot, the MARS group, in their search for new ideals in architecture. Later, at the height of his popularity, he did not immerse himself, even as President of The Royal Institute of British Architects, in the burning social issues of the day remaining as one commentator put it 'politically innocent'.[5] By instinct he preferred to design buildings without the need for social or communal dogma. When he sought to address the needs of

RIAS

The careful framing of Reid's Court, Canongate, Edinburgh, shows Spence's sensitivity to historic buildings, though there are also bold new elements in the design of the buildings.

Like Lutyens, Spence was not always popular with his professional contemporaries for many of the same reasons. Indifferent to contemporary radical agendas both Lutyens and, later, Spence stood apart from the changing architectural 'zeitgeist' and followed their own personal design development.

working-class housing in Glasgow, his response was to romanticise the tenement, to indulge his fancy as a maker of monuments. Spence, like the critic Herbert Read, saw art as a grand expression of social realities.

Neither a natural delegator nor an architect who readily compromised his initial design concept, Spence rapidly (and usually independently) reached the basis of a design which then grew *'like a plant from a single stem'*. Though faced by hostility at Coventry he never contemplated fundamental change. With the Gorbals flats he persisted with a concept, which, with hindsight, was clearly unsuited to climate and social need. His relationship with his partners was not as equals, at least as far as design was concerned. Spence worked largely alone on competition entries, preparing drawings which would have taken his assistants three times as long to produce. His partners' role was to be supportive and helpful, translating drawings into buildings as long as they did not change the initial idea. This reluctance to defer to others, to compromise and his inability to delegate contributed to an increasing isolation and, latterly, unpopularity.

As Spence's career progressed his early interest in craftsmanship and regional architecture gave way to a growing maturity in the handling of light, space and matter. An interest in the traditional and organic declined as Spence explored expressive and monumental forms – rather as Edwin Lutyens' career had done. He too had established his practice on designing and building English houses in the Arts and Crafts tradition, before moving to a freely composed and monumental Classicism. As with Lutyens, Spence's interior and exterior were closely related entities, sharing a common concern for light and procession. Whereas Lutyens pursued the *'High Game'* of late Classicism, Spence explored what he called the *'lusher pastures of plastic expression'* implicit in modern architecture. At Glasgow Airport, Edinburgh University Library and Mortonhall Crematorium, the interior volumes and the expressive exterior structure, were united by a rigorous application of principles which were essentially artistic in spirit.

There are comparisons with two other twentieth-century British architects. One, James Stirling, who had roots, at least partly, in the Scottish building tradition, developed from a regionally translated modern architecture towards an architecture of sculptural illumination, procession and building volume. While Stirling's forms are curvilinear and angular, Spence's are largely orthogonal. Secondly, Eric Lyons' buildings have similar sculptural qualities to those of Spence. Lyons, believing that Spence was *'grossly misjudged and unfairly criticised'* praised the architect for *'creating richness and visual diversity'*.[6] Both Stirling and Lyons shared with Spence an aptitude to use light as a material in its own right, a

RIAS

Swan Chair designed by Spence for Princess Anne in December 1950. The architect's facility for witty furniture design recalls that of his former master Edwin Lutyens.

Thurso High School, 1958.

substance to punctuate neutral planes and give meaning and direction to architectural space.

Spence realised that his designs would never appeal to everybody. He had an artist's conviction in the appropriateness of his concepts and defended them tenaciously; yet he was deeply sensitive and strangely insecure for a man who had won so many honours and designed such an impressive portfolio of buildings. The insecurity, rarely visible but to close friends, was generally hidden behind a mask of self-confidence, sartorial style and oratory.

At the height of his powers, the work rate of Spence was phenomenal. He entered many architectural competitions winning about a quarter of them. When he was short-listed by clients, his persuasive powers and artistic flair resulted in his firm's appointment rather than those of his competitors. He worked alone on competitions, often through the night, adding his own letraset and annotating the plans with neat freehand notes. One of his partners reported that Spence probably did alone in three weeks what would normally take five people.[7] His speed of thought and fluency of hand provided the cement for the growing practice in Edinburgh and then London. Spence was the leader of an 'atelier' as much as an office and had, in his prime, the same authority and quickness of manner which he had experienced at the hands of Lutyens.

The currents and cross-currents of taste rarely displaced Spence who remained remarkably true to a handful of principles. Pre-eminent among the precepts, was the importance of context – what he would have called 'genius loci'. To Spence the task of the architect was to be a new shoot on an old tree, not a new tree altogether. His buildings grew from a combination of tradition expressed in modern spirit and a sensitivity to a specific location. The brilliance of his design at Coventry lay in his exploitation of the shell of the bombed cathedral as an approach to the new building and in

For Spence an architecture of reductionist principles and minimalist aesthetics failed to respond adequately to the wider demands of site, climate, geography, cultural and artistic traditions. Deriving his early experiences of architecture from Scotland where such concerns are paramount, Spence was able to take to England – and latterly abroad – an architecture which resonated with a sense of context, both physical and cultural.

the adoption of the structural rhythms of the old building. At a local scale the success of his Dunbar housing lies in the interpretation of the heritage of the fishing burgh into modern buildings and spaces that still suited contemporary housing needs. This empirical approach to design is even more evident in the Canongate flats where crispness and visual austerity hint at the difficulty of being truly a new modern shoot on a very ancient tree. At Sussex and Edinburgh Universities the demands of new functions are met by new forms carefully attuned to place, climate and tradition. In 1939 Spence declared that buildings should be *'direct and simple in* [their] *conception with an eye for proportion and an understanding use of materials'*.[8] Though his later buildings became more powerful and sculptural, these principles guided a lifetime's design.

It is time to review the work of Basil Spence, particularly after the demolition of his Gorbals flats in 1993. In the realm of art and architecture he remains poorly understood and insufficiently appreciated. Many of his buildings stand inadequately maintained or face the prospect of refurbishment which will alter the distinctive character Spence imposed. Though robust in spirit, his buildings have not always been robust in construction or supported by clients appreciative of their value. Glasgow Airport has been disastrously engulfed in a plastic embrace which has suffocated the beauty of the original. Where he sought *'unity, control, honesty and sincerity'*,[9] others have been caught in the fashionable deceit of restyling the products of an earlier age. As Eric Lyons said, Spence's major public buildings *'reflected the spirit of vitality and enthusiasm that was shared by the British people in the post-war era'*.[10] Lyons also remarked that the *'architects of any period cannot be adequately assessed by their contemporaries'* but he was certain that the status of Spence would be recognised by future generations.[11]

Sea and Ships pavilion at the Festival of Britain, 1951.

Notes

Notes to Introduction

1. Obituary: Basil Spence by Richard Sheppard. *RIBA Journal*, January 1977.
2. Ibid.
3. Ibid.
4. *The Brave New World: Scotland Rebuilt 1945-1970.* Exhibition catalogue by Miles Glendinning, Ranald MacInnes and David Page, 1993.
5. 'Tribute to a Scottish Monumentality', James Dunnett. *Building Design*, 6 August 1993.
6. Basil Spence, *Phoenix at Coventry.* Geoffrey Bles, London, 1962, p13.
7. Ibid., p28.
8. 'The Architect of Controversy', Judy Hillman. *The Guardian,* 20 November 1976.
9. Ibid.
10. Ibid.
11. Ibid.
12. Obituary: Sir Basil Spence. *The Daily Telegraph,* 20 November 1976.
13. *Op cit.,* note 4, p12.
14. Peter Fawcett, Essay on Basil Spence in *International Dictionary of Architects and Architecture.* St James Press, Detroit, **1**, p852.
15. Lionel Esher, *A Broken Wave: The Rebuilding of England 1940-1980.* Allen Lane, London, 1981, p66.

Notes to Chapter One

1. For information on Spence's time at George Watson's I am indebted to Mr F E Gerstenberg, Principal of the College.
2. Edinburgh College of Art, student appliction file, 1925-6.
3. Personal communication from Richard Ewing, son-in-law of William Kininmonth.
4. For Edinburgh College of Art records on Spence I am indebted to Professor Alistair Rowan, Principal, for tracing Spence and his achievements through the College register. His maintenance bursary was &40. Marks were 100% for design work but 54% for building construction.
5. Christopher Hussey, *The Life of Sir Edwin Lutyens.* Country Life Ltd, 1950, p556.
6. Personal communication with Neil Parkyn based upon an interview with Basil Spence in 1965.
7. A E Richardson and Hector Corfiato, *The Art of Architecture.* The English Universities Press Ltd, 1938, p256.
8. Personal communication with Anthony Blee, Spence's son-in-law, on 23 March 1994.
9. *Scottish Architecture 1930-40:* Architect Interviews (Sir William Kininmonth). RIAS, Thirties File.
10. Laurence Wodehouse, 'Old Guard, Avant-Garde'. *Building Design*, **434**, 23 February 1979, p28-9.
11. Basil Spence, 'Tradition in Scottish Architecture'. *Building Industries,* April 1939, p13.
12. The quote relayed by Lady Christine Erskine-Hill refers to a chance remark by Spence made during an unexpected encounter at a restaurant in London.
13. Ledger Book, **2**, p315, Rowand Anderson, Paul & Partners office records.
14. Michael Hanson, *A Spence House in Stirlingshire.* Country Life, August 9, 1984.
15. Here I am indebted to Lady Erskine-Hill, a second cousin of the Colvilles and regular visitor to Gribloch.
16. *The Times,* 20 November 1976.
17. Ledger Book, **1**, p469, Rowand Anderson, Paul & Partners
18. Charles McKean, *The Scottish Thirties: An Architectural Introduction.* 1987, p186.
19. Sidney Rogerson, 'Glasgow: ICI at the Exhibition'. *ICI Magazine,* May 1938, p394.
20. Ibid.
21. McKean, *op cit.,* p187.
22. Wodehouse, *op cit.,* p29.
23. Basil Spence, 'Tradition in Scottish Architecture'. *Building Industries,* April 1939, p13.
24. Basil Spence, 'Constructional Methods and Materials', Misha Black (Ed). *Exhibition Design,* London, 1950, p114.
25. McKean, *op cit.,* p142.
26. S.R.O., B18.13.19: Dunbar Council Minutes.

Notes to Chapter Two

1. Personal communication with Richard Ewing, 22 January 1993.
2. Personal communication with Hardie Glover, 7 December 1992.
3. *The Glasgow Herald,* 27 December 1948.
4. Ibid.
5. Basil Spence, 'Constructional Methods and Materials', Misha Black (Ed). *Exhibition Design,* London, 1950, p114.
6. Personal communication with Jim Beveridge, 7 December 1992.
7. University of Glasgow, *Court Minutes.* 1946-47, p67.
8. University of Glasgow, *Court Records*, 51260A.
9. Ibid.
10. University of Glasgow, Building File BE/3/2, letter and report dated 1 November 1948.

Notes to Chapter Three

1. Basil Spence, *Phoenix at Coventry.* London, 1962, p3.
2. A full account of the design and construction of the school is in *RIAS Quarterly.* **3**, Autumn 1956.
3. Principal's address, 4 December 1955. University of Edinburgh Development Committee, **1**, 1954-56.
4. Minutes of University of Edinburgh Development Committee, 11 March 1954.
5. Minutes of University of Edinburgh Development Committee, 29 November 1954.
6. Ibid.
7. Ibid.
8. Edinburgh Corporation, Planning Committee Minutes, 13 July 1955.
9. *The Times,* 20 November 1976.
10. Basil Spence, 'Building a New University', in David Daiches, *The Idea of a New University.* London, 1964, p203.
11. Basil Spence, *Phoenix at Coventry.* London, 1962, p11.
12. Peter Fawcett, Essay on Basil Spence in *International Dictionary of Architects and Architecture.* St James Press, Detroit, **1**, p852.
13. Lewis Mumford is quoted in the obituary to Basil Spence in *The Daily Telegraph*, 20 November 1976. See also *New Yorker,* 10 March 1962.
14. Edward Mills, 'Cathedrals and Churches by Basil Spence', *The Architect and Building News,* 2 May 1958, p672.

Notes to Chapter Four

1. *The Architects' Journal,* 4 September 1958, p326.
2. Personal communication with the job architect Charles Robertson, 24 November 1992.
3. *The Architects' Journal,* 4 September 1958, p326.
4. Miles Horsey, *Tenements and Towers: Glasgow Working-Class Housing 1890-1990.* Edinburgh, 1990, p39.
5. Personal communication with William Dickson, 5 January l993.
6. Personal communication with Hardie Glover, 2 April 1993.
7. *The Architects' Journal,* 8 June 1966, p8.
8. A J Youngson, *Urban Development and the Royal Fine Art Commissions.* Edinburgh University Press, 1990, p127.

Notes to Chapter Five

1. *The Times,* 20 November 1976.
2. Basil Spence, 'The Cathedral Church of St Michael, Coventry'. *RIBA Journal,* February 1955, p145.
3. Basil Spence, 'Tradition in Scottish Architecture'. *Building Industries,* April 1939, p9.
4. *Op cit.,* note 1.
5. Lionel Esher, *A Broken Wave: The Rebuilding of England 1940-1980.* Allen Lane, London, 1981, p65.
6. 'The Architect of Controversy'. *The Guardian,* 20 November 1976.
7. Ibid.
8. Basil Spence, 'Tradition in Scottish Architecture'. *Building Industries,* April 1939, p13.
9. Ibid., p13.
10. *The Scotsman,* 20 November 1976.
11. Ibid.

SIR BASIL SPENCE (1907-1976)
Born
Bombay, India, of Scottish parents, 13 August 1907
Father: Urwin Spence of Orkney descent
Mother: Daisy Crisp
Died: Eye, Suffolk, 19 November 1976

Education
George Watson's College, Edinburgh 1919-25
Edinburgh College of Art 1925-9 1930-1
Bartlett School of Architecture, London University
(under Albert Richardson 1929: evening classes)

Student Prizes
RIAS Incorporation Prize 1928
RIBA Recognised Schools Silver Medallist 1931
Arthur Cates Prize 1932 (Joint winner with Sir
Robert Matthew)
Pugin Student Prize 1933

Training/Apprenticeship
Sir Edwin Lutyens' office (London)
1929-30 worked on Viceroy's House, New Delhi
Assistant to Rowand Anderson, Paul & Partners,
Edinburgh 1931-5

Services
British Army Camouflage Unit 1939-44 (Major)
Staff Captain (Intelligence) 1944-45

Academic Posts
Part-time lecturer Edinburgh College of Art 1931-9,
1945-46
Hoffman Wood Professor of Architecture,
University of Leeds 1955-57
Professor of Architecture, Royal Academy
(London) 1961-8

Practice
Entered practice (1931-5) with William Kininmonth
(loose association) whilst in Rowand Anderson's
Office, Practice address, 16 Rutland Sq, Edinburgh
Freelance perspectivist 1928-1937
1935 appointed partner in Rowand Anderson, Paul
and Partners.
Basil Spence and Partners 1946-51
Spence, Glover and Ferguson, Edinburgh 1951-1992
Spence, Bonnington and Collins, London 1952-1992

Family
Married: Mary Joan Ferris (1934); 2 children, Milton
and Gillian

Professional
Fellow, RIBA 1947, President RIBA 1958-60
Associate, Royal Scottish Academy 1952
Associate, Royal Academy (London) 1953
Royal Academician 1960
Royal Designer for Industry 1960 (one of 50
appointed)

RIBA Bronze Medal 1963 (for Falmer House,
University of Sussex)
Hon Fellow, American Institute of Architects 1963
Hon Member, Academia di San Luca, Rome 1973
Board of Trustees, Civic Trust 1967-72

Other Honours/Posts
Awarded OBE 1948, TD 1959, KBE
1960, RA 1960, OM 1962
Festival of Britain Award for Housing 1951
Member, Royal Fine Art Commission (E & W) 1956-
70
Grand Medaille d'Or Academie d'Architecture,
Paris 1974
Hon Fellow, Royal College of Art, London 1962
Honorary degrees, Southampton 1965, Leicester
1963, Manitoba 1963

LIST OF PROJECTS
Town Planning

consultant	University of Southampton	1960
consultant	University of Sussex	1960-64
consultant	University of Edinburgh	1955-60
consultant	University of Nottingham	1955-60
consultant	Basildon New Town	1962

Work Achievements

1932	House at 6 Castlelaw Road, Colinton for Sir James Allan
1932	Burnmouth Housing Scheme (James Berry: RIAS Collection)
1933	Causewayside Garage, Edinburgh (3 perspectives RIAS Collection)
1933	Glenburn House, Glenlockhart, Edinburgh (attributed to William Kininmonth)
1933	Double villa for Mrs Williamson (Elevation and Plans: NMRS)
1934	Lismhor, 11 Easter Belmont Road, Edinburgh (for Dr King)
1934	Houses in Comiston Estate, Edinburgh including 220 Braid Road, 15 Braid Hills Ave (for Dr Watson 1934)
1934	House for Mrs Spence (Mother), 6 Comiston Rise (Braid Estate), Edinburgh
1934	Deaconess Hospital, Edinburgh (Assisted A F Balfour Paul)
1935	House for Miss Reid, 4 Easter Belmont Road, Edinburgh
1935	Row of houses, Victoria Road, Dunbar
1935	House, 57 Oxgangs Road, Edinburgh (Elevation and Plans: NMRS)
1935	Church (unidentified) (perspective: NMRS)
1935	Building Exhibition, Waverley Market, Edinburgh
1936	Scottish pavilion, Johannesburg Exhibition
1936	Edinburgh Dental Hospital (Assisted A F Balfour Paul)
1936	Liberton House, near Edinburgh, re-casing
1936	Broughton Place, Peebles (for Professor

	Elliot), now Broughton Gallery (perspectives: NMRS)
1936	House for Mr L H Brennan, 141 Corsebar Road, Paisley
1937	Scottish School of Art & Industry, Kilsyth (won in competition, 1937 : partly built 1938-39)
1937	Cleghorn's, George St (now Pearl Assurance) Edinburgh
1937	Corstorphine Church restoration and alterations (Assisted A F Balfour Paul)
1938	Quothquhan, near Biggar (for Sir Alexander G and Lady Eskine-Hill, MP, now owned by Tony Jacklin)
1938	Nurses home, Falkirk (with Kininmonth)
1938	Scottish pavilion, ICI Building, Country House for the Council for Art and Industry, all at the Empire Exhibition Glasgow. (Spence attributes the Scottish pavilion *in collaboration with Thomas Tait*)
1938	Gribloch for John Colville near Kippen, Stirlingshire (with Perry Duncan of New York)
1939	Housing, Forth (with Kininmonth)
1946	Restoration and extension of house in Bell's Brae, Edinburgh (for Alexander Zyw)
1946-48	Housing, Bannerfield, Selkirk
1947-49	Adviser: Board of Trade for British Industries Fair
1947	'Britain Can Make It' Exhibition, Olympia, London as Chief Architect
1947	Enterprise Scotland Exhibition, Edinburgh
1947-51	Natural Philosophy building, Glasgow University
1948	ICI pavilion, Copenhagen Exhibition
1949	Scottish Industries Exhibition, Glasgow (Kelvin Hall)
1949-51	Range of furniture design in laminated timber, mahogany and hide for Morris of Glasgow (selection now in the Museum of Modern Art, New York)
1950	Housing at harbourside, Dunbar Harbour
1950	Board Room furniture design for Scottish Furniture Manufacturers Ltd
1950	Swan Chair design for Princess Anne
1950-51	Housing, Sunbury-on-Thames, Surrey
1951	Unrealised design for St Ninian and St Martin's Church, Whithorn, Scotland
1951	Housing, Shepperton, Middlesex
1951	Heavy Industries Exhibition, Sea and Ships pavilion, The Skylark Restaurant, Nelson Pier, all at the Festival of Britain, London
1951	Coventry Cathedral Competition won
1951	Spence moves to London
1952	ICI pavilion, Copenhagen Exhibition
1952	Pulpit, Crossford Church, Lanarkshire

List of projects

1952	Duncanrig Secondary School, East Kilbride
1954	Ecclesfield Secondary Modern School, Sheffield, Yorkshire
1954	Comprehensive School, Sydenham, London
1955	Parsons Cross Secondary School, Sheffield
1955	St Andrew's Church, Clermiston, Scotland
1955	The Cottage, Gosford Road, Longniddry
1956	Shopping Centre, East Kilbride (unrealised)
1956	Restoration of Plewlands House, South Queensferry
1956	University of Durham, Physics Building
1956-60	Main Operating Theatres and Laundry, Western General Hospital, Edinburgh
1957	SAI fertiliser works, Leith
1957	Flats, Newhaven, Edinburgh (Saltire Award)
1957	St Martin's School, near Shrewsbury, Shropshire
1957	St Chad's Church, Bell Green, St Oswalds Church, Tile Hill and Church of St John the Divine, Willenhall, Coventry (3 churches for Bishop Gorton)
1958	St Paul's Church, Ecclesfield, Yorkshire (see school above)
1958	Slough Town Hall
1958	St Catherine's Church, Woodthorpe, Sheffield, Yorkshire
1958	Consultant Architect, Basildon New Town, Essex
1958	Housing, Oxlease Estate, Hatfield, Hertfordshire
1958	Wray House, Wimbledon, London
1958	Thurso High School
1959	2nd Extension, Natural Philosophy building, Glasgow University
1959	St Aidan's Church, Leicester
1959	Boardroom, Grosvenor Place, London
1959	Thorn House, St Martin's Lane, London (with Andrew Renton)
1959	Research and Teaching Building, University of Liverpool
1960	Undergraduate Residence, Queen's College, Cambridge
1960	Physics Building, University of Liverpool
1960	Institute of Virology, University of Glasgow
1960	Aeronautics and Mechanical Engineering Building, Glen Eyre Residences and Economics Building, University of Southampton
1960	House at 27 Merchiston Gardens, Edinburgh for headmaster of George Watson's School
1960	Physics Building, University of Newcastle
1960	Trinity College, Glenalmond, Perthshire
1961	St Francis Church, Newall Green, Wythershawe, Lancashire

1961	Spence House, Beaulieu, Hampshire
1961	Agriculture Building, University of Newcastle
1962	Design Consultant, BOAC hangar, Heathrow (with Sir Frederick Snow & Partners)
1962	Cathedral of St Michael, Coventry (won in competition 1951)
1962	Scottish Widows Fund & Life Assurance Society Building, 9-10 St Andrew Square, Edinburgh
1962	Procter & Gamble Building, Newcastle
1962	Power Station, Trawsfynydd, Wales (concept design & consultant)
1962	Housing II, Basildon New Town, Essex
1962	High-rise housing, Gorbals, Glasgow
1962	Senior Common Room, University of Southampton
1962	Falmer House, University of Sussex
1964	Animal Breeding Research Building, University of Edinburgh
1963	Arts Building, University of Southampton
1963	Chemistry Building, University of Southampton
1964	Hampstead Civic Centre
1964	2 homes, Banalbufar, Majorca
1964	Nuffield Theatre, University of Southampton
1964	Civil and Engineering Building, University of Southampton
1964	Library Phase 1, University of Sussex
1965	Chemistry Building, University of Exeter
1965	Chemistry Building, University of Sussex
1965	St Aidan's Chapel, University of Durham
1966	Canongate Housing, Royal Mile, Edinburgh
1966	Crematorium, Mortonhall, Edinburgh
1966	Dept of Genetics, Glasgow University
1966	Terminal, Glasgow Airport (destroyed in remodelling of 1991)
1966	Meeting House, University of Sussex
1966	Students Union Building, University of Southampton
1966	James Clark Maxwell Building, University of Edinburgh
1966	Physics Building, University of Southampton
1966	Animal House, University of Southampton
1966	Lecture Theatre, University of Exeter
1967	Library and Staff Club, University of Edinburgh
1967	British pavilion, Expo '67 (Montreal)
1967	Swimming Pool, Campden (design only)
1967	Physics Building, University of Exeter
1967	Geology/Botany Building, University of Southampton
1967	Crookfur Cottage Homes, Newton Mearns, Glasgow
1967	Physics Building, University of Sussex
1967	St Matthew's Church, Reading, Berkshire
1968	Albyn Restaurant, Queen Street, Edinburgh

1969	Municipal Library, Newcastle-upon-Tyne
1969	All Saints office redevelopment, Newcastle-upon-Tyne (consultant)
1969	Tizard Building extension, University of Southampton
1969	Recreation Building, University of Sussex
1969	Biology Building, University of Sussex
1970	Household Cavalry Barracks, Knightsbridge
1970	Satellite Pier, Glasgow Airport (realised in reduced form)
1970	Town Hall and Civic Centre, Sunderland
1970	House, Fawwara, Malta
1970	Boathouse and Exhibition Hall, Carmel College, Mongewell, Oxfordshire
1970	Institute of Development Studies, University of Sussex
1971	Chancery, British Embassy, Rome
1971	Bridge, Gateshead
1971	Rivierstaete Building, Amsterdam (consultant)
1971	Library (Phase II), University of Sussex
1972	Royal Infirmary, Glasgow
1972	Queen's College, Cambridge (consultant)
1972	Heriot-Watt University Library
1972	Scottish Widows Fund & Life Assurance Society Headquarters, Dalkeith Road, Edinburgh
1972	Administration Building, University of Sussex
1973	Zoology Building, University of Southampton
1974	Parliament Building extension, Wellington, New Zealand (original design and consultant)
1974	Palais des Nations extension, Geneva (as consultant with Professor Nervi)
1975	Bank of Piraeus, Athens (consultant)
1975	International Airport, Baghdad (consultant)
1975	Northampton Lodge, Canonbury, London
1975	Arts Building, University of Sussex
1975	Geology and Mining Building, University of Newcastle
1975	University College Library, Dublin
1976	Invited competition design, Cultural Centre Bahrein
1976	Queen Anne's Mansions office development, Victoria, London, original design and consultant
1976	Kensington and Chelsea Civic Centre
1976	Mariposa Luxury Apartments, Cannes
1976	Ionian Popular Bank, Piraeus (consultant)

References and Index

REFERENCES

Contemporary Architects Ed. Muriel Emanuel, Macmillan Press Ltd, 1980

To Build a Cathedral (catalogue, 1987), Louis Campbell, University of Warwick

The Scottish Thirties Charles McKean, Scottish Academic Press 1987

Index to Architects RIBA Library Architect Files NMRS

Basil Spence Exhibition catalogue (Jane Thomas) RIAS 1992

Books (by Spence)

Exhibition Design, Chapter by Spence in Misha Black (ed), London, 1950.

The Cathedral of St Michael, Coventry, London, 1962.

Phoenix at Coventry: The Building of a Cathedral, London, 1962.

Out of the Ashes: A Progress Through Coventry Cathedral, with Henk Snoek, London, 1963.

The Idea of a New University: An Experiment in Sussex, with others, edited by David Daiches, London, 1964.

New Buildings in Old Cities, Southampton, 1973.

Books (on Spence in part)

Broken Wave: The Rebuilding of England 1940-80 by Lionel Esher, London 1981.

The Scottish Thirties, Charles McKean, Scottish Academic Press, 1987.

Contemporary Architects Ed: Muriel Emanuel, Macmillan Press Ltd, London, 1980.

New Architecture in Scotland Peter Willis, London, 1977.

International Dictionary of Architecture and Architects essay on Basil Spence by Peter Fawcett, vol 1, pp852-5, St James Press, Detroit, 1993.

Building the New Universities, Tony Birks, Newton Abbot, 1972.

Articles (by Spence)

'Tradition in Scottish Architecture' in *Building Industries*, pp9-12, April 1939.

'The Modern Church' in *RIBA Journal*, July 1956.

Articles (on Spence)

'Basil Spence' in *The Observer* (London), 14 June 1959.

'The Very Model of a Monumental

O.M.' by Peter Lewis in *Queen*, 4 December 1962.

'Sir Basil Spence' by Lewis Mumford in *New Yorker*, 10 March 1962.

'Pillar of Architecture' by David Pryce-Jones in *Telegraph Magazine*, 28 September 1973.

'Obituary' by Richard Sheppard in *RIBA Journal*, January 1977.

'Obituary' by Sir Frederick Gibberd in *Architectural Review*, April 1977.

'Sir Basil Spence: An Architect's Appreciation' by Colin Campbell in *Scottish Review* (Edinburgh), Spring 1977.

'Old Guard, Avant-Garde' by Lawrence Wodehouse, *Building Design*, 23 February 1979.

'Basil Spence in the Thirties' by Louise Campbell in *RIBA Journal*, April 1993, pp32-35.

'Appreciation of Basil Spence', Robert Scott Morton, 1966 typescript ms. NMRS.

Catalogues

To Build a Cathedral Louis Campbell, University of Warwick, 1987.

Basil Spence Jane Thomas, RIAS Publications, Edinburgh, 1992.

Biographies:

AJ	1951	5 July	p7
AR	1955	Jan	p76
AR	1956	Jan	p76
AJ	1958	3 July	p2
(Presidential address)			

Obituaries

RIBA Journal January 1977

Architectural Review April 1977

Scottish Review (Edinburgh) Spring 1977

Newspaper obituaries The Times, The Daily Telegraph, The Guardian etc 20 November 1976

Drawing Collections

RIAS Spence Collection (lodged at NMRS)

RIBA Drawings Collection (limited value)

University of Glasgow and Mackintosh School (mainly Gribloch drawings)

William Kininmonth (Richard Ewing) Collection (NMRS)

RIAS James Berry Collection

Photographic Archive

Deposit of office drawings and photographs to RIAS in 1992 by Jim Beveridge

Index